THE 21 IRREFUTABLE
LAWS OF
LEADERSHIP
WORKBOOK

BOOKS BY DR. JOHN C. MAXWELL
CAN TEACH YOU HOW TO BE A REAL SUCCESS

RELATIONSHIPS

Be a People Person

Becoming a Person of Influence

Relationships 101

The Power of Partnership in the Church

The Treasure of a Friend

Ethics 101

Winning with People

25 Ways to Win with People

Encouragement Changes Everything

ATTITUDE

Be All You Can Be

Failing Forward

The Power of Thinking Big

Living at the Next Level

Think on These Things

Your Bridge to a Better Future

The Power of Attitude

Attitude 101

Thinking for a Change

The Difference Maker

The Journey from Success to Significance

EQUIPPING

Developing the Leaders Around You

Equipping 101

The 17 Indisputable Laws of Teamwork

The 17 Essential Qualities of a Team Player

Partners in Prayer

Your Road Map for Success

Success One Day at a Time

Today Matters

Talent Is Never Enough

The Choice is Yours

LEADERSHIP

The 21 Indispensable Qualities of a Leader

Revised & Updated 10th Anniversary
Edition of *The 21 Irrefutable Laws of Leadership*

The 21 Most Powerful Minutes in a Leader's Day

Developing the Leader Within You

Leadership 101

Leadership Promises for Every Day

Leadership Promises for Your Week

The 360 Degree Leader

The Right to Lead

The Power of Leadership

Leadership Gold (Spring 2008)

THE 21 IRREFUTABLE LAWS OF LEADERSHIP WORKBOOK

FOLLOW THEM *and* PEOPLE WILL FOLLOW YOU

REVISED & UPDATED
10TH ANNIVERSARY EDITION

JOHN C. MAXWELL

THOMAS NELSON
Since 1798

NASHVILLE   DALLAS   MEXICO CITY   RIO DE JANEIRO   BEIJING

Published in Nashville, Tennessee, by Thomas Nelson. Thomas Nelson is a trademark of Thomas Nelson, Inc.

Thomas Nelson, Inc. titles may be purchased in bulk for educational, business, fund-raising, or sales promotional use. For information, please e-mail SpecialMarkets@ThomasNelson.com.

Scripture quotations noted CEV are from THE CONTEMPORARY ENGLISH VERSION. © 1991 by the American Bible Society. Used by permission.

Scripture quotations noted *The Message* are from *The Message: The New Testament in Contemporary English.* Copyright © 1993 by Eugene H. Peterson.

ISBN: 978-1-4185-2615-3

Printed in the United States of America
18 19 20   LSC   32

CONTENTS

1. THE LAW OF THE LID   1

Leadership Ability Determines a Person's Level of Effectiveness

Brothers Dick and Maurice came as close as they could to living the American Dream—without making it. Instead a guy named Ray did it with the company they had founded. It happened because they didn't know the Law of the Lid.

2. THE LAW OF INFLUENCE   13

The True Measure of Leadership Is Influence—Nothing More, Nothing Less

Abraham Lincoln started with the rank of captain, but by the time the war was over, he was a private. What happened? He was a casualty of the Law of Influence.

3. THE LAW OF PROCESS   23

Leadership Develops Daily, Not in a Day

Theodore Roosevelt helped create a world power, won a Nobel Peace Prize, and became president of the United States. But today you wouldn't even know his name if he hadn't known the Law of Process.

4. THE LAW OF NAVIGATION   33

Anyone Can Steer the Ship, but It Takes a Leader to Chart the Course

Using a fail-safe compass, Scott led his team of adventurers to the end of the earth—and to inglorious deaths. They would have lived if only he, their leader, had known the Law of Navigation.

CONTENTS

INTRODUCTION

Every book is a conversation between the author and the individual reading it. Some people pick up a book hoping for a bit of encouragement. Some devour a book's information as if they were attending an intensive seminar. Others find in its pages a mentor they can meet with on a daily, weekly, or monthly basis.

The thing I love about writing books is that it allows me to "talk" to many people I will never personally meet. That's why I made the decision in 1977 to become an author. I had a passion to add value to people that energized me to write. That passion still burns within me today. Few things are more rewarding to me than being on the road and having someone I've never met approach me to say, "Thank you. Your books have really helped me." It's why I write—and intend to continue writing!

Despite the deep satisfaction of knowing that my books help people, there is also a great frustration that comes with being an author. Once a book is published, it freezes in time. If you and I knew each other personally and we met weekly or monthly to talk about leadership, every time we got together I'd share with you something new I'd learned. As a person, I continue to grow. I'm constantly reading. I'm analyzing my mistakes. I'm talking to excellent leaders to learn from them. Each time you and I were to sit down, I'd say, "You won't believe what I just learned."

As a conference and event speaker, I often teach the principles I write about in my books, and I'm constantly updating my material. I use new stories. I refine ideas. And I often gain new insights as I stand in front of an audience. However, when I go back to books that I've written previously, I first become aware of how I've changed since I've written them. But second, I become frustrated because the books can't grow and change along with me.

That's why I got excited when my publisher, Thomas Nelson, asked if I would like to revise *The 21 Irrefutable Laws of Leadership* for a special tenth anniversary edition. When I originally wrote the book and workbook, they were my answer to the question, "If you were to take everything you've learned about leadership over the years and boil it down into a short list, what would it be?" I put on paper the essentials of leadership, communicated as simply and clearly as possible. And soon after the book was published and it appeared on four different best-seller lists, I realized it had the potential to help a lot of people become better leaders.

GROWTH = CHANGE

But now, years later, there are things I am no longer satisfied with in the original edition. I knew I could improve upon some ideas in the original edition. Some stories had become dated, and I wanted to replace them with new ones. I had also developed new material to better explain and illustrate some of the ideas. While teaching the laws for nearly a decade in dozens of countries around the world, I fielded thousands of questions about the laws. That process advanced my thinking beyond what it was when I first wrote *The 21 Irrefutable Laws of Leadership*. Working on this tenth anniversary edition has allowed me to make those improvements.

By far the biggest change I wanted to make to the original book centered on two of the laws.

"What?" you may ask. "How can you *change* one of your *irrefutable* laws?"

First of all, while teaching them I soon discovered that two of the laws were really just subsets of other laws. The Law of E. F. Hutton (When the Real Leader Speaks, People Listen) was really just an aspect of the Law of Influence (The True Measure of Leadership Is Influence—Nothing More, Nothing Less). When people around a table stop and listen to a leader speak, they are revealing that the speaker has influence. Because the ideas in the Law of E. F. Hutton were part of the Law of Influence, I merged those two chapters. Similarly, I recognized that the Law of Reproduction (It Takes a Leader to Raise Up a Leader) was assumed in the Law of Explosive Growth (To Add Growth, Lead Followers—To Multiply, Lead Leaders). For that reason, I combined them as well.

The other thing that happened was that I began to realize that I had missed some things when writing about the laws of leadership originally. The first omission I discovered as soon as I had taught the laws a few times in developing countries. I found that in many of those places, leadership was focused on position, privilege, and power. In my paradigm of leadership, I took some things for granted. I see leadership primarily as a form of service and had never identified a law to teach that principle. The second oversight had to do with modeling leadership and impacting the culture of an organization. The result is the inclusion of two new laws in this tenth anniversary edition of *The 21 Irrefutable Laws of Leadership:*

The Law of Addition: Leaders Add Value by Serving Others
The Law of the Picture: People Do What People See

From today's perspective I ask myself, *How could I have missed them?* But I did. The good news is that you won't! I feel certain that these two laws will add immeasurably to your ability to lead. Serving others and showing others the way are two critical components of successful leadership. I wish I could revise each of my books every ten years to include things I missed!

MORE LESSONS LEARNED

There are two other things I've been reminded of as I've taught the 21 Laws these last ten years:

1. LEADERSHIP REQUIRES THE ABILITY TO DO MORE THAN ONE THING

Instinctively, successful people understand that focus is important to achievement. But leadership is very complex. During a break at a conference where I was teaching the 21 Laws, a young college student came up to me and said, "I know you are teaching 21 Laws of Leadership, but I want to get to the bottom line." With intensity, he raised his index finger and asked, "What is the one thing I need to know about leadership?"

Trying to match his intensity, I raised my index finger and answered, "The one thing you need to know about leadership is that there is more than one thing you need to know about leadership!" To lead well, we must do 21 things well.

2. No One Does All 21 Laws Well

Despite the fact that we must do 21 things well to be excellent leaders, it is reality that none of us does all of them well. For example, I am average or below average in five of the laws—and I wrote the book! So what is a leader to do? Ignore those laws? No, develop a leadership team.

At the beginning of this workbook there is a leadership evaluation. I encourage you to take it to evaluate your aptitude for each law. Once you've discovered in which laws you are average or below, begin looking for team members whose skills are strong where yours are weak. They will complement you and vice versa, and the whole team will benefit. That will make it possible for you to develop an all-star leadership team. Remember, none of us is as smart as all of us.

SOME THINGS NEVER CHANGE

Though I have made adjustments to the laws and updated the ways I teach them, some things have not changed in the last ten years. It's still true that leadership is leadership, no matter where you go or what you do. Times change. Technology marches forward. Cultures differ from place to place. But the principles of leadership are constant—whether you're looking at the citizens of ancient Greece, the Hebrews in the Old Testament, the armies of the modern world, the leaders in the international community, the pastors in local churches, or the businesspeople of today's global economy. Leadership principles are unchanging and stand the test of time.

As you read the following chapters, I'd like you to keep in mind four ideas:

1. **The laws can be learned.** Some are easier to understand and apply than others, but every one of them can be acquired.
2. **The laws can stand alone.** Each law complements all the others, but you don't need one in order to learn another.

3. **The laws carry consequences with them.** Apply the laws, and people will follow you. Violate or ignore them, and you will not be able to lead others.
4. **These laws are the foundation of leadership.** Once you learn the principles, you have to practice them and apply them to your life.

Whether you are a follower who is just beginning to discover the impact of leadership or a natural leader who already has followers, you can become a better leader. As you read and answer questions about the laws, you may recognize that you already practice some of them very effectively. Other laws may expose weaknesses you didn't know you had. Use your review as a learning experience. The questions and exercises are included to help you apply each law to your life.

You can certainly learn the laws of leadership on your own using this workbook. However, since leadership is about working with people, this workbook has been set up so that groups can learn about the laws together. The first three sections in each chapter (Read, Observe, Learn) are to be completed individually, and the last three sections (Discuss, Apply, Action) are most effective if reviewed in a group setting. Since individuals have different strengths and weaknesses, if you work together on each law, you will learn from each other. *Before you get started working through the chapters, I recommend that you take the leadership evaluation*, which you will find on the next few pages. That will give you a benchmark of where you are starting in the leadership growth process. Then when you are done with this workbook, complete the evaluation again.

No matter where you are in the leadership development process, know this: the greater the number of laws you learn, the better leader you will become. Each law is like a tool, ready to be picked up and used to help you achieve your dreams and add value to other people. Pick up even one, and you will become a better leader. Learn them all, and people will gladly follow you.

Now, let's open the toolbox together.

21 Laws Leadership Evaluation

Read each statement below and score yourself for each, using the following scale:

0 Never
1 Rarely
2 Occasionally
3 Always

1. The Law of the Lid

Leadership Ability Determines a Person's Level of Effectiveness

a) When faced with a challenge, my first thought is, *Who can I enlist to help?* not *What can I do?*

b) When my team, department, or organization fails to achieve an objective, my first assumption is that it's some kind of leadership issue.

c) I believe that developing my leadership skills will increase my effectiveness dramatically.

TOTAL

2. The Law of Influence

The True Measure of Leadership Is Influence—Nothing More, Nothing Less

a) I rely on influence rather than on my position or title to get others to follow me or do what I want.

b) During discussions or brainstorming settings, people turn to me and ask for my advice.

c) I rely on my relationships with others rather than organizational systems and procedures to get things done.

TOTAL

3. THE LAW OF PROCESS
Leadership Develops Daily, Not in a Day

a) I have a concrete, specific plan for personal growth that I engage in weekly.

b) I have found experts and mentors for key areas of my life with whom I engage on a regular basis.

c) To promote my professional growth, I have read at least six books (or taken at least one worthwhile class or listened to twelve or more audio lessons) per year for the last three years.

TOTAL

4. THE LAW OF NAVIGATION
Anyone Can Steer the Ship, but It Takes a Leader to Chart the Course

a) I spot problems, obstacles, and trends that will impact the outcome of initiatives the organization puts into place.

b) I can clearly see a pathway for the implementation of a vision, including not only the process but also the people and resources needed.

c) I am called upon to plan initiatives for the department or organization.

TOTAL

5. THE LAW OF ADDITION
Leaders Add Value by Serving Others

a) Rather than being annoyed when team members have issues preventing them from doing their jobs effectively, I see the issues as an opportunity to serve and help those people.

b) I look for ways to make things better for the people I lead.

c) I find great personal satisfaction in helping other people become more successful.

TOTAL

6. THE LAW OF SOLID GROUND

Trust Is the Foundation of Leadership

a) The people I lead confide in me regarding sensitive issues.

b) When I tell someone in the organization that I will do something, he can count on me to follow through.

c) I avoid undermining others or talking behind their backs.

TOTAL

7. THE LAW OF RESPECT

People Naturally Follow Leaders Stronger Than Themselves

a) People are naturally drawn to me and often want to do things with me just to spend time with me.

b) I go out of my way to show respect and loyalty to the people I lead.

c) I make courageous decisions and take personal risks that could benefit my followers even if there is no benefit to me.

TOTAL

8. THE LAW OF INTUITION

Leaders Evaluate Everything with a Leadership Bias

a) I can easily gauge morale, whether in a room full of people, on a team, or in an organization.

b) I often take the right action as a leader even if I cannot explain why.

c) I can read situations and sense trends without having to gather hard evidence.

TOTAL

9. THE LAW OF MAGNETISM

Who You Are Is Who You Attract

    a) I am satisfied with the caliber of people who report to me.

    b) I expect the people I attract to be similar to me in values, skills, and leadership ability.

    c) I recognize that no personnel process can improve the quality of people I recruit compared to improving myself.

TOTAL

10. THE LAW OF CONNECTION

Leaders Touch a Heart Before They Ask for a Hand

    a) When I am new to a leadership situation, one of the first things I try to do is to develop a personal connection with the individuals involved.

    b) I know the stories, hopes, and dreams of the people I lead.

    c) I avoid asking people to help accomplish the vision until we have built a relationship that goes beyond the nuts and bolts of our work together.

TOTAL

11. THE LAW OF THE INNER CIRCLE

A Leader's Potential Is Determined by Those Closest to Him

    a) I am strategic and highly selective about which people are closest to me personally and professionally.

    b) I regularly rely on some key people in my life to help accomplish my goals.

    c) I believe that 50 percent or more of the credit for my accomplishments goes to the people on my team.

TOTAL

12. THE LAW OF EMPOWERMENT

Only Secure Leaders Give Power to Others

a) I embrace change easily and become dissatisfied with the *status quo.*

b) I believe that no matter how talented the people who work for me are, my position is secure.

c) It is my regular practice to give people I lead the authority to make decisions and take risks.

TOTAL

13. THE LAW OF THE PICTURE

People Do What People See

a) If I observe an undesirable action or quality in team members, I check for it in myself first before addressing it with them.

b) I am continually working to try to make my actions and words consistent with one another.

c) I do what I should rather than what I want because I am conscious that I am setting an example for others.

TOTAL

14. THE LAW OF BUY-IN

People Buy into the Leader, Then the Vision

a) I recognize that a lack of credibility can be as harmful to an organization as a lack of vision.

b) I wait until I see that most of the people on the team have confidence in me before asking for a commitment to the vision.

c) Even when my ideas are not very good, my people tend to side with me.

TOTAL

15. THE LAW OF VICTORY
Leaders Find a Way for the Team to Win

a) When I lead a team, I feel ultimate responsibility for whether it achieves its goals.

b) If members of my team are not unified in their efforts to achieve the vision, I take action to get them on the same page.

c) I make personal sacrifices to help ensure victory for my team, department, or organization.

TOTAL

16. THE LAW OF THE BIG MO
Momentum Is a Leader's Best Friend

a) I am enthusiastic and maintain a positive attitude every day for the sake of my team members.

b) Whenever I make a major leadership decision, I consider how that decision will impact momentum in my team, department, or organization.

c) I initiate specific actions with the purpose of generating momentum when introducing something new or controversial.

TOTAL

17. THE LAW OF PRIORITIES
Leaders Understand That Activity Is Not Necessarily Accomplishment

a) I avoid tasks that are not required by my leadership, don't have a tangible return, or don't reward me personally.

b) I set aside time daily, monthly, and yearly to plan my upcoming schedule and activities based on my priorities.

c) I delegate any task for which a team member can be at least 80 percent as effective as I could be.

TOTAL

18. THE LAW OF SACRIFICE
A Leader Must Give Up to Go Up

a) I know making trade-offs is a natural part of leadership growth, and I make sacrifices to become a better leader as long as they don't violate my values.

b) I expect to give more than my followers do in order to accomplish the vision.

c) I will give up my rights in order to reach my potential as a leader.

TOTAL

19. THE LAW OF TIMING
When to Lead Is As Important As What to Do and Where to Go

a) I expend as much effort figuring out the timing for an initiative as I do figuring out the strategy.

b) I will launch something using a less-than-ideal strategy because I know the timing is right.

c) I can sense whether or not people are ready for an idea.

TOTAL

20. THE LAW OF EXPLOSIVE GROWTH
To Add Growth, Lead Followers—To Multiply, Lead Leaders

a) I believe that I can grow my organization more rapidly by developing leaders than by any other method.

b) I spend a significant amount of time every week investing in the development of the top 20 percent of my leaders.

c) I would rather see leaders I develop succeed out on their own than keep them with me so that I can keep mentoring them.

TOTAL

21. THE LAW OF LEGACY

A Leader's Lasting Value Is Measured by Succession

a) I possess a strong sense of why I am in my job and why I am leading.

b) In each position I've held, I have identified people who can carry on after me, and I have invested in them.

c) One of my strongest motivations is to leave any team I lead better than I found it.

TOTAL

Now that you have completed the evaluation, examine each law and note your strengths and weaknesses. Use the following guidelines to help you proceed.

8–9   This law is in your strength zone. Make the most of this skill and mentor others in this area.

5–7   Target this law for growth. You have potential to make it a strength.

0–4   This is a weakness. Hire staff with this strength or partner with others in this area.

1

THE LAW OF THE LID

Leadership Ability Determines a Person's Level of Effectiveness

T HE LAW OF THE LID WILL HELP YOU UNDERSTAND THE VALUE OF LEAD-ERship. If you can get a handle on this law, you will see the incredible impact of leadership on every aspect of life.

> ## READ

In 1930, two young brothers named Dick and Maurice moved from New Hampshire to California in search of the American Dream. They had just gotten out of high school, and they saw few opportunities back home. So they headed straight for Hollywood where they eventually found jobs on a movie studio set.

After a while, their entrepreneurial spirit and interest in the entertainment industry prompted them to open a theater in Glendale, a town about five miles northeast of Hollywood. But despite all their efforts, the brothers just couldn't make the business profitable. In the four years they ran the theater, they weren't able to consistently generate enough money to pay the one hundred dollars a month rent that their landlord required.

The brothers' desire for success was strong, so they kept looking for better business opportunities. In 1937, they finally struck on something that worked. They opened a small drive-in restaurant in Pasadena, located just east of Glendale. People in Southern California had become very dependent on their cars, and the culture was changing to accommodate that, including its businesses.

The drive-in restaurant was a phenomenon that sprang up in the early thirties, and it was becoming very popular. Rather than being invited into a dining room to eat, customers would drive into a parking lot around a small restaurant, place their orders with carhops, and receive their food on trays right in their cars. The food was served on china plates complete with glassware and metal utensils. It was a timely idea in a society that was becoming faster paced and increasingly mobile.

Dick and Maurice's tiny drive-in restaurant was a great success, and in 1940, they decided to move the operation to San Bernardino, a working-class boomtown fifty miles east of Los Angeles. They built a larger facility and expanded their menu from hot dogs, fries, and shakes to include barbecued beef and pork sandwiches, hamburgers, and other items. Their business exploded. Annual sales reached $200,000, and the brothers found themselves splitting $50,000 in profits every year—a sum that put them in the town's financial elite.

In 1948, their intuition told them that times were changing, and they made modifications to their restaurant business. They eliminated the carhops and started serving only walk-up customers. And they also streamlined everything. They reduced their menu and focused on selling hamburgers. They eliminated plates, glassware, and metal utensils, switching to paper products instead. They reduced their costs and lowered the prices they charged customers. They also created what they called the Speedy Service System. Their kitchen became like an assembly line, where each employee focused on service with speed. The brothers' goal was to fill each customer's order in thirty seconds or less. And they succeeded. By the mid-1950s, annual revenue hit $350,000, and by then, Dick and Maurice split net profits of about $100,000 each year.

Who were these brothers? Back in those days, you could have found out by driving to their small restaurant on the corner of Fourteenth and E Streets in San Bernardino. On the front of the small octagonal building hung a neon sign that said simply MCDONALD'S HAMBURGERS. Dick and Maurice McDonald had hit the great American jackpot, and the rest, as they say, is history, right? Wrong. The McDonalds never went any farther because their weak leadership put a lid on their ability to succeed.

It's true that the McDonald brothers were financially secure. Theirs was one of the most profitable restaurant enterprises in the country, and they felt that they had a hard time spending all the money they made. Their genius was in customer service and kitchen organization. That talent led to the creation of a new system of food and beverage service. In fact, their talent was so widely known in food service circles that people started writing them and visiting from all over the country to learn more about their methods. At one point, they received as many as three hundred calls and letters every month.

That led them to the idea of marketing the McDonald's concept. The idea of franchising restaurants wasn't new. It had been around for several decades. To the McDonald brothers, it looked like a way to make money without having to open another restaurant themselves. In 1952, they got started, but their effort was a dismal failure. The reason was simple. They lacked the leadership necessary to make a larger enterprise effective. Dick and Maurice were good single-restaurant owners. They understood how to run a business, make their systems efficient, cut costs, and increase profits. They were efficient managers. But they were not leaders. Their thinking patterns clamped a lid down on what they could do and become. At the height of their success, Dick and Maurice found themselves smack-dab against the Law of the Lid.

In 1954, the brothers hooked up with a man named Ray Kroc, who was a leader. Kroc had been running a small company he founded, which sold machines for making milk shakes. He knew about McDonald's. The restaurant was one of his best customers. And as soon as he visited the store, he had a vision for its potential. In his mind he could see the restaurant going nationwide in hundreds of markets. He soon struck a deal with Dick and Maurice, and in 1955, he formed McDonald's Systems, Inc. (later called the McDonald's Corporation).

Kroc immediately bought the rights to a franchise so that he could use it as a model and prototype. He would use it to sell other franchises. Then he began to assemble a team and build an organization to make McDonald's a nationwide entity. He recruited and hired the sharpest people he could find, and as his team grew in size and ability, his people developed additional recruits with leadership skill.

In the early years, Kroc sacrificed a lot. Though he was in his mid-fifties, he worked long hours just as he had when he first got started in business thirty years earlier. He eliminated many frills at home, including his country club membership, which he later said added ten strokes to his golf game. During his first eight years with McDonald's, he took no salary. Not only that, but he personally borrowed money from the bank and against his life insurance to help cover the salaries of a few key leaders he wanted on the team. His sacrifice and his leadership paid off. In 1961 for the sum of $2.7 million, Kroc bought the exclusive rights to McDonald's from the brothers, and he proceeded to turn it into an American institution and global entity. The "lid" in the life and leadership of Ray Kroc was obviously much higher than that of his predecessors.

In the years that Dick and Maurice McDonald had attempted to franchise their food service system, they managed to sell the concept to just fifteen buyers, only ten of whom actually opened restaurants. And even in that size enterprise, their limited leadership and vision were hindrances. For example, when their first franchisee, Neil Fox of Phoenix, told the brothers that he wanted to call his restaurant McDonald's, Dick's response was, "What . . . for? McDonald's means nothing in Phoenix."

In contrast, the leadership lid in Ray Kroc's life was sky high. Between 1955 and 1959, Kroc succeeded in opening 100 restaurants. Four years after that, there were 500 McDonald's. Today the company has opened more than 31,000 restaurants in 119 countries.[1]

OBSERVE

Leadership ability is the lid that determines a person's level of effectiveness. The lower an individual's ability to lead, the lower the lid on his potential. The higher the individual's ability to lead, the higher the lid on his potential.

Leadership ability—or more specifically the lack of leadership ability—was the lid on the McDonald brothers' effectiveness.

1. *Give two examples of steps Ray Kroc took to build the franchise business that the McDonald bothers didn't take.*

_____

_____

_____

_____

2. *How did these actions reflect Ray Kroc's leadership ability?*

_____

_____

_____

3. *From your profession or area of service, give an example of a leader who has been limited by his or her "lid." How has this leader's "lid" affected the organization?*

_____

_____

_____

4. *Do you know someone whose leadership lid seems unlimited?*

_____

_____

_____

LEARN

Whatever you will accomplish is restricted by your ability to lead others. For example, if your leadership rates an 8, then your effectiveness can never be greater than a 7. If your leadership is only a 4, then your effectiveness will be no higher than a 3. Your leadership ability—for better or for worse—always determines your effectiveness and the potential impact of your organization.

Let me give you an example of what I mean. Let's say that when it comes to success, you're an 8 (on a scale from 1 to 10). That's pretty good. I think it would be safe to say that the McDonald brothers were in that range. But let's also say that leadership isn't even on your radar. You don't care about it, and you make no effort to develop as a leader. You're functioning as a 1. Your level of effectiveness would look like this:

SUCCESS WITHOUT LEADERSHIP

LEADERSHIP ABILITY

EFFECTIVENESS

SUCCESS DEDICATION

To increase your level of effectiveness, you have a couple of choices. You could work very hard to increase your dedication to success and excellence—to work toward becoming a 10. It's possible that you could make it to that level, though the Law of Diminishing Returns says that the effort it would take to increase those last two points might take more energy than it did to achieve the first eight. If you really killed yourself, you might increase your success by that 25 percent.

But you have another option. You can work hard to increase your level of *leadership*. Let's say that your natural leadership ability is a 4—slightly below average. Just by using whatever God-given talent you have, you already increase your effectiveness by 300 percent. But let's say you become a real student of leadership and you maximize your potential. You take it all the way up to a 7. Visually, the results would look like this:

By raising your leadership ability—without increasing your success dedication at all—you can increase your original effectiveness by 600 percent. Leadership has a multiplying effect.

DISCUSS

Answer the following questions and discuss your answers when you meet with your team.

1. *How effective will a person be if he increases his leadership but not his work ethic (dedication to success)?*

_____

_____

_____

2. *Do you agree with the author's assessment that increasing your leadership is one of the best ways to increase your level of effectiveness? Explain.*

_____

_____

_____

3. *What criteria can be used to determine a person's leadership ability? What are some clear signs of leadership strengths and weaknesses?*

_____

_____

_____

4. *How long does it take you to determine a person's leadership "lid" once that person has been put in charge of a team?*

_____

_____

_____

5. *Describe signs indicating that a leader has hit his or her lid.*

_____

_____

_____

6. *Describe a situation in which your leadership lid negatively affected a project or task.*

_____

_____

_____

7. *On a scale of 1 to 10, how would you describe your leadership? Would your spouse or colleagues agree with your assessment?*

_____

_____

_____

8. *Up to now, how dedicated have you been to developing yourself as a leader? How will you increase that dedication?*

_____

_____

_____

APPLY

1. List some of your major goals. (Try to focus on significant objectives—things that will require a year or longer of your time. List at least five but no more than ten items.) Now identify which ones will require the participation or cooperation of other people. For these activities, your leadership ability will greatly impact your effectiveness.

2. Assess your leadership ability. Review the leadership assessment you took at the start of this workbook to get an idea of your basic leadership ability.

3. Ask others to rate your leadership. Talk to your boss, your spouse, two colleagues (at your level), and three people you lead about your leadership ability. Ask each of them to rate you on a scale of 1 (low) to 10 (high) in each of the following areas:

- People skills
- Planning and strategic thinking
- Vision
- Results

Average the scores, and compare them to your own assessment. Based on these assessments, is your leadership skill better or worse than you expected? If there is a gap between your assessment and that of others, what do you think is the cause? How willing are you to grow in the area of leadership?

TAKE ACTION

Interview someone whom you consider to have a high leadership lid. Ideally this would be the person you listed in the OBSERVE section for: Whom do you know whose leadership lid seems unlimited? Ask that person the following questions:

1. *When did you first see yourself as a leader?*

   _____

   _____

   _____

2. *What are some of the greatest challenges you've faced as a leader?*

   _____

   _____

   _____

3. *What has contributed to your growth as a leader?*

   _____

   _____

   _____

4. *What are you currently doing to grow as a leader?*

   _____

   _____

   _____

5. *What is the best piece of advice that you would have for someone who aspires to be an effective leader?*

_____

_____

_____

2

THE LAW OF INFLUENCE

The True Measure of Leadership Is Influence—
Nothing More, Nothing Less

I f you don't have influence, you will *never* be able to lead others. As psychologist Harry A. Overstreet observed, "The very essence of all power to influence lies in getting the other person to participate." If no one is following you, you're not a leader. The *Law of Influence* is about obtaining followers, which makes it the basis for leadership.

READ

One of my favorite stories that illustrates the Law of Influence concerns Abraham Lincoln. In 1832, decades before he became president, young Lincoln gathered together a group of men to fight in the Black Hawk War. In those days, the person who put together a volunteer company for the militia often became its leader and assumed a commanding rank. In this instance, Lincoln was given the rank of captain. But Lincoln had a problem. He knew nothing about soldiering. He had no prior military experience, and he knew nothing about tactics. He had trouble remembering the simplest military procedures.

For example, one day Lincoln was marching a couple of dozen men across a field and needed to guide them through a gate into another field. But he couldn't manage it. Recounting the incident later, Lincoln said, "I could not for the life of me remember the proper word of command for getting my company endwise. Finally, as we came near [the gate] I shouted: 'This company is dismissed for two minutes, when it will fall in again on the other side of the gate.'"1

As time went by, Lincoln's level of influence with others in the militia actually *decreased*. While other officers proved themselves and gained rank, Lincoln found himself going in the other direction. He began as a captain, but *title and position* did him little good. He couldn't overcome the Law of Influence. By the end of his military service, Abraham Lincoln had found his rightful place, having achieved the rank of private.

Fortunately for Lincoln—and for the fate of the United States—he overcame his inability to influence others. Lincoln followed his time in the military with undistinguished stints in the Illinois state legislature and the U.S. House of Representatives. But over time and with much effort and personal experience, he became a person of remarkable influence and impact, and one of the nation's finest presidents.

I love the leadership proverb that says, "He who thinks he leads, but has no followers, is only taking a walk." If you can't influence people, then they will not follow you. And if people won't follow, you are not a leader. That's the Law of Influence. No matter what anybody else may tell you, remember that leadership is influence—nothing more, nothing less.

OBSERVE

Leadership is often misunderstood. When people hear that someone has an impressive title or an assigned leadership position, they assume that individual to be a leader. Sometimes that's true. But titles don't have much value when it comes to leading. True leadership cannot be awarded, appointed, or assigned. It comes only from influence, and that cannot be mandated. It must be earned. The only thing a title can buy is a little time—either to increase your level of influence with others or to undermine it.

1. *Why was Lincoln an ineffective captain?*

_____

_____

_____

2. *How did Lincoln's inability to influence others affect his military career?*

_____

_____

_____

3. *What is the most basic factor you can use to determine if someone is a leader or not?*

_____

_____

_____

4. *According to the definition "leadership is influence," who are the most prominent leaders in your industry? What influence do they have over industry trends and standards?*

_____

_____

_____

5. *Within your organization, who is not formally recognized as a leader, but has influence over others?*

_____

_____

_____

LEARN

There are plenty of misconceptions and myths that people embrace about leaders and leadership. Here are five common ones:

1. THE MANAGEMENT MYTH

A widespread misunderstanding is that leading and managing are one and the same. Up until a few years ago, books that claimed to be on leadership were often really about management. The main difference between the two is that leadership is about influencing people to follow, while management focuses on maintaining systems and processes. As former Chrysler chairman and CEO Lee Iacocca wryly commented, "Sometimes even the best manager is like the little boy with the big dog, waiting to see where the dog wants to go so that he can take him there."

The best way to test whether a person can lead rather than just manage is to ask him to create positive change. Managers can maintain direction, but often they can't change it. Systems and processes can do only so much. To move people in a new direction, you need influence.

2. The Entrepreneur Myth

Frequently, people assume that all entrepreneurs are leaders. But that's not always the case. Entrepreneurs are skilled at seeing opportunities and going after them. They see needs and understand how to meet them in a way that produces a profit. But not all of them are good with people. Many find it necessary to partner with someone skilled at the people part of the equation. If they can't influence people, they can't lead.

3. The Knowledge Myth

Sir Francis Bacon said, "Knowledge is power." If you believe power to be the essence of leadership, then you might naturally assume that those who possess knowledge and intelligence are therefore leaders. That isn't necessarily true. You can visit any major university and meet brilliant research scientists and philosophers whose ability to think is so high that it's off the charts, but whose ability to lead is so low that it doesn't even register on the charts. Neither IQ nor education necessarily equates to leadership.

4. The Pioneer Myth

Another misconception is that anyone who is out in front of the crowd is a leader. But being first isn't always the same as leading. For example, Sir Edmund Hillary was the first man to reach the summit of Mount Everest. Since his historic ascent in 1953, hundreds of people have "followed" him in achieving that feat. But that doesn't make Hillary a leader. He wasn't even the official leader on the expedition when he reached the summit. John Hunt was. And when Hillary traveled to the South Pole in 1958 as part of the Commonwealth Trans-Antarctic Expedition, he was accompanying another leader, Sir Vivian Fuchs. To be a leader, a person has to not only be out front, but also have people intentionally coming behind him, following his lead, and acting on his vision. Being a trendsetter is not the same as being a leader.

5. THE POSITION MYTH

As mentioned earlier, the greatest misunderstanding about leadership is that people think it is based on position, but it's not. Think about what happened several years ago at Cordiant, the advertising agency formerly known as Saatchi & Saatchi. In 1994, institutional investors of Saatchi and Saatchi forced the board of directors to dismiss Maurice Saatchi, the company's CEO. What was the result? Several executives followed him out. So did many of the company's largest accounts, including British Airways and Mars, the candy maker. Saatchi?s influence was so great that his departure caused the company?s stock to fall immediately from $8 5⁄8 to $4 per share.[2] What happened is a result of the Law of Influence. Saatchi lost his title and position, but he continued to be the leader. Stanley Huffty affirmed, "It's not the position that makes the leader; it's the leader that makes the position."

Although people in your organization may buy into one of these myths, when all is said and done, true leadership is influence. Leadership is the ability to obtain followers. It is the ability to influence others to follow you. Because without followers, who are you leading?

DISCUSS

Answer the following questions and discuss your answers when you meet with your team.

1. *What is the difference between management and leadership?*

   _____

   _____

   _____

2. *Do you agree with the author's assessment that leadership is influence? Explain.*

_____

_____

_____

3. *What obstacles might people come up against if they have bought into one of the leadership myths?*

_____

_____

_____

4. *Describe a situation when you were part of a team that was led by a person who was placed in charge because of his knowledge or position and not his leadership abilities.*

_____

_____

_____

5. *Would you consider yourself to be a leader? Whom do you influence?*

_____

_____

_____

6. *What are some positive ways you could expand your influence in your organization?*

_____

_____

_____

APPLY

1. Which of the myths in the chapter have you bought into in the past: management, entrepreneur, knowledge, pioneer, or position? Why have you been susceptible to that myth? What does that say about your perception of leadership up until now? What must you change in your current thinking to make you more open to improving your leadership in the future?

2. What do you usually rely upon most to persuade people to follow you? Rate yourself on a scale of 1 to 10 for each of the seven factors named in the chapter (a 1 means it's not a factor while a 10 means you rely on it continually):

Character—who you are
Relationships—who you know
Knowledge—what you know
Intuition—what you feel
Experience—where you've been
Past success—what you've done
Ability—what you can do

How can you optimize or better utilize the ones with low scores?

3. Find an organization for which to volunteer. Pick something you believe in—a school, soup kitchen, community project, and so on—and offer your time and energy. If you believe you have leadership ability, then try leading. You will learn to lead through influence.

TAKE ACTION

This week, try to influence five people: a supervisor, a colleague on your same position level, a follower in your sphere of influence, a follower outside of your sphere of influence, and a family member or close friend. It could be as simple as suggesting where to go eat, or as critical as suggesting a new direction for a project. At the end of the week, review each situation by following the instructions noted.

Superior: _____

My expectation: Result and Explanation:

_____   _____

_____   _____

_____   _____

_____   _____

Colleague—on same position level: _____

My expectation: Result and Explanation:

_____   _____

_____   _____

_____   _____

_____   _____

Follower—in your area of influence: _____

My expectation: Result and Explanation:

_____   _____

_____   _____

_____   _____

_____   _____

Follower—not in your area of influence: _____

My expectation: Result and Explanation:

_____   _____

_____   _____

_____   _____

_____   _____

Family member or close friend: _____

My expectation: Result and Explanation:

_____   _____

_____   _____

_____   _____

_____   _____

In what instances were you successful in influencing others to go along with your idea? Put a + next to these occurrences.

In what instances were you unsuccessful in influencing others to go along with your idea? Put a (✓) next to these occurrences.

For each situation evaluate why you expected someone to follow your lead. Was it because: you were in a position of authority; you were the most knowledgeable person on the subject; you were the person who came up with the original idea; you were the recognized leader? Then evaluate why you think people did or did not follow your lead.

When do you find yourself being influenced by someone else because of his or her position, knowledge or leadership?

_____

_____

_____

How is that similar to the way people have responded to you?

_____

_____

_____

3

THE LAW OF PROCESS

Leadership Develops Daily, Not in a Day

BECOMING A LEADER IS A LOT LIKE INVESTING SUCCESSFULLY IN THE STOCK market. If your hope is to make a fortune in a day, you're not going to be successful. There are no successful "day traders" in leadership development. What matters most is what you do day by day over the long haul.

READ

There is an old saying: champions don't become champions in the ring—they are merely recognized there. That's true. If you want to see where someone develops into a champion, look at his daily routine. Former heavyweight champ Joe Frazier stated, "You can map out a fight plan or a life plan. But when the action starts, you're down to your reflexes. That's where your road work shows. If you cheated on that in the dark of the morning, you're getting found out now under the bright lights."[1] Boxing is a good analogy for leadership development because it is all about daily preparation. Even a person with natural talent has to prepare and train to become successful.

One of this country's greatest leaders was a fan of boxing: President Theodore Roosevelt. In fact, one of his most famous quotes uses a boxing analogy:

> It is not the critic who counts, not the man who points out how the strong man stumbled, or where the doer of deeds could have done them better. The credit

belongs to the man who is actually in the arena; whose face is marred by dust and sweat and blood; who strives valiantly; who errs and comes short again and again; who knows the great enthusiasms, the great devotions, and spends himself in a worthy cause; who, at best, knows in the end the triumph of high achievement; and who, at the worst, if he fails, at least fails while daring greatly, so that his place shall never be with those cold and timid souls who know neither victory nor defeat.

Roosevelt, a boxer himself, was the ultimate man of action. Not only was he an effective leader, but he was one of the most flamboyant of all U.S. presidents. British historian Hugh Brogan described him as "the ablest man to sit in the White House since Lincoln; the most vigorous since Jackson; the most bookish since John Quincy Adams."

TR (Roosevelt's nickname) is remembered as an outspoken man of action and proponent of the vigorous life. While in the White House, he was known for regular boxing and judo sessions, challenging horseback rides, and long, strenuous hikes. A French ambassador who visited Roosevelt used to tell about the time that he accompanied the president on a walk through the woods. When the two men came to the banks of a stream that was too deep to cross by foot, TR stripped off his clothes and expected the dignitary to do the same so that they could swim to the other side. Nothing was an obstacle to Roosevelt.

At different times in his life, Roosevelt was a cowboy in the Wild West, an explorer and big-game hunter, and a rough-riding cavalry officer in the Spanish-American War. His enthusiasm and stamina seemed boundless. As the vice presidential candidate in 1900, he gave 673 speeches and traveled 20,000 miles while campaigning for President McKinley. And years after his presidency, while preparing to deliver a speech in Milwaukee, Roosevelt was shot by a would-be assassin. With a broken rib and a bullet in his chest, Roosevelt insisted on delivering his one-hour speech before allowing himself to be taken to the hospital.

Of all the leaders this nation has ever had, Roosevelt was one of the toughest— both physically and mentally. But he didn't start that way. America's cowboy president was born in Manhattan to a prominent wealthy family. As a child, he was puny and very sickly. He had debilitating asthma, possessed very poor eyesight, and was painfully thin. His parents weren't sure he would survive.

When he was twelve, young Roosevelt's father told him, "You have the mind, but you have not the body, and without the help of the body the mind cannot go as far as it should. You must *make* the body." Make it he did. He lived by the Law of Process.

TR began spending time *every day* building his body as well as his mind, and he did that for the rest of his life. He worked out with weights, hiked, ice-skated, hunted, rowed, rode horseback, and boxed. In later years, Roosevelt assessed his progress, admitting that as a child he was "nervous and timid. Yet," he said, "from reading of the people I admired . . . and from knowing my father, I had a great admiration for men who were fearless and who could hold their own in the world, and I had a great desire to be like them."[2] By the time TR graduated from Harvard, he *was* like them, and he was ready to tackle the world of politics.

Roosevelt didn't become a great leader overnight, either. His road to the presidency was one of slow, continual growth. As he served in various positions, ranging from New York City police commissioner to president of the United States, he kept learning and growing. He improved himself, and in time he became a strong leader. That was further evidence that he lived by the Law of Process.

Roosevelt's list of accomplishments is remarkable. Under his leadership, the United States emerged as a world power. He helped the country develop a first-class navy. He saw that the Panama Canal was built. He negotiated peace between Russia and Japan, winning a Nobel Peace Prize in the process. And when people questioned TR's leadership—since he had first become president when McKinley was assassinated—he campaigned and was reelected by the largest majority of any president up to his time.

Ever the man of action, when Roosevelt completed his second term as president in 1909, he immediately traveled to Africa where he led a scientific expedition sponsored by the Smithsonian Institution. A few years later, in 1913, he co-led a group to explore the uncharted River of Doubt in Brazil. It was a learning adventure he said he could not pass up. "It was my last chance to be a boy," he later admitted. He was fifty-five years old.

On January 6, 1919, at his home in New York, Theodore Roosevelt died in his sleep. Then Vice President Marshall said, "Death had to take him sleeping, for if Roosevelt had been awake, there would have been a fight." When they removed him from his bed, they found a book under his pillow. Up to the very last, TR was still striving to learn and improve himself. He was still practicing the Law of Process.

If you want to be a leader, the good news is that you can do it. Everyone has the potential, but it isn't accomplished overnight. It requires perseverance. And you absolutely cannot ignore the Law of Process. Leadership doesn't develop in a day. It takes a lifetime.

OBSERVE

My friend Tag Short maintains, "The secret of our success is found in our daily agenda." If you continually invest in your leadership development, letting your "assets" compound, the inevitable result is growth over time.

1. *What are some of the challenges Roosevelt had to overcome in order to become a great leader?*

   _____

   _____

   _____

2. *What are some things Roosevelt included in his daily agenda that contributed to his leadership ability?*

   _____

   _____

   _____

3. *Roosevelt looked to his father and other leaders he read about for inspiration. Who are some of the people you look to for inspiration? Why?*

   _____

   _____

   _____

4. *Whom do you admire in your profession or area of service? Why is this person inspirational?*

_____

_____

_____

5. *Whom in your profession or area of service do you think could have achieved more than he or she did? Why do you think this person settled for less? How does this person's dedication to personal growth factor into his or her level of success?*

_____

_____

_____

6. *Which person from questions four and five do you more identify with? Why?*

_____

_____

_____

LEARN

In a study of ninety top leaders from a variety of fields, leadership experts Warren Bennis and Burt Nanus made a discovery about the relationship between growth and leadership: "It is the capacity to develop and improve their skills that distinguishes leaders from their followers." Successful leaders are learners. And the learning process is ongoing, a result of self-discipline and perseverance. The goal each day must be to get a little better, to build on the previous day's progress.

Whether or not you possess great natural ability for leadership, your development and progress will probably occur according to the following five phases:

PHASE 1: I DON'T KNOW WHAT I DON'T KNOW
Many people fail to recognize the value of leadership. Some don't recognize its

importance. Others believe that leadership is only for a few—for the people at the top of the corporate ladder. They have no idea of the opportunities they're passing up when they don't learn to lead. This point was driven home for me when a college president shared with me that only a handful of students signed up for a leadership course offered by the school. Why? Only a few thought of themselves as leaders. If they had understood that leadership is influence, and that in the course of each day most individuals usually try to influence at least four other people, their desire might have been sparked to learn more about the subject. It's unfortunate because as long as a person doesn't know what he doesn't know, he isn't going to grow.

PHASE 2: I KNOW THAT I NEED TO KNOW

At some point in life, many people find themselves placed in a leadership position only to look around and discover that no one is following them. When that happens, we realize that we need to *learn* how to lead. And of course, that's when it's possible for the process to start. English Prime Minister Benjamin Disraeli wisely commented, "To be conscious that you are ignorant of the facts is a great step to knowledge."

That's what happened to me when I took my first leadership position in 1969. I had captained sports teams all my life and had been the student government president in college, so I already thought I was a leader. But when I tried to lead people in the real world, I found out the awful truth. Being put in charge is not the same as being a leader.

PHASE 3: I KNOW WHAT I DON'T KNOW

I struggled for a while in that first leadership position. To be honest, I relied on my extremely high energy and whatever charisma I possessed. But there came a moment when I realized that leadership was going to be the key to my professional career. If I didn't get better at leadership, my career would eventually bog down, and I would never reach the goals I had set for myself. Fortunately at that time, I had breakfast with Kurt Kampmeir of Success Motivation, Inc. At that breakfast, he asked a question that would change my life.

"John," he asked, "what is your plan for personal growth?"

I fumbled for an answer and then finally admitted that I didn't have one. That night my wife, Margaret, and I decided to make financial sacrifices so that I could get on the program Kurt offered. That was an intentional step toward growth. From that day to now, I have made it a practice to read books, listen to tapes, and go to conferences on leadership.

Around the time I met with Kurt, I also had another idea: I wrote to the top ten leaders in my field and offered them one hundred dollars for a half hour of their time so that I could ask them questions. (That was quite a sum for me back then.) For the next several years, Margaret and I planned every vacation around where those people lived. If a great leader in Cleveland said yes to my request, then that year we vacationed in Cleveland so that I could meet him. I can't explain how valuable those experiences were for me. Those leaders shared insights with me that I could have learned no other way.

PHASE 4: I KNOW AND GROW, AND IT STARTS TO SHOW

When you recognize your lack of skill and begin the daily discipline of personal growth, exciting things start to happen.

Several years ago I was teaching leadership to a group of people in Denver, and in the crowd I noticed a really sharp nineteen-year-old named Brian. For a couple of days, I watched as he eagerly took notes. I observed him interacting with others. And I talked to him a few times during breaks. When I got to the part of the seminar where I teach the Law of Process, I asked Brian to stand up so that I could talk to him, and I wanted everyone else in the audience to listen in.

"Brian, I've been watching you here," I said, "and I'm very impressed with how hungry you are to learn and glean and grow. I want to tell you a secret that will change your life." Everyone in the whole auditorium seemed to lean forward.

"I believe that in about twenty years, you can be a *great* leader. I want to encourage you to make yourself a lifelong learner of leadership. Read books, listen to tapes regularly, and keep attending seminars. And whenever you come across a golden nugget of truth or a significant quote, file it away for the future.

"It's not going to be easy," I said. "But in five years, you'll see progress as your influence becomes greater. In ten years, you'll develop a competence that makes your leadership highly effective. And in twenty years, when you're only thirty-nine years old, if you've continued to learn and grow, others will likely start asking you to teach them about leadership. And some will be amazed. They'll look at each other and say, 'How did he suddenly become so wise?'

"Brian," I concluded, "you can be a great leader, but it won't happen in a day. Start paying the price now." What's true for Brian is also true for you. Start developing your leadership today, and someday you will experience the effects of the Law of Process.

Phase 5: I Simply Go Because of What I Know

When you're in phase four, you can be pretty effective as a leader, but you have to think about every move you make. However, when you reach phase five, your ability to lead becomes almost automatic. You develop great instincts. And that's when the payoff is incredible. But the only way to get there is to obey the Law of Process and pay the price.

DISCUSS

Answer the following questions and discuss your answers when you meet with your team.

1. *According to the Law of Process, what must you be committed to in order to become a successful leader?*

   _____

   _____

   _____

2. *Do you agree with the author that leadership is a process? Why or why not?*

   _____

   _____

   _____

3. *Is leadership only for a few people? Why?*

   _____

   _____

   _____

4. *What steps do you see the other leaders in your organization taking in order to become better leaders?*

_____

_____

_____

5. *A year ago, which of the Five Phases would you have placed yourself in? Why? How about today?*

_____

_____

_____

6. *In the last year what has contributed the most to your growth as a leader?*

_____

_____

_____

APPLY

1. What is your personal plan for growth? If you are like I was when Kurt Kampmeir asked me this question, you have a vague intention to grow, not a specific plan. Write out a plan. I recommend that you read one book a month, listen to at least one CD, tape, or streaming message a week, and attend one conference a year. Select the materials in advance, set aside time for growth on your calendar, and start immediately. If developing a plan from scratch seems difficult, you may want to read my book *Today Matters*. It contains the personal growth plan I have used for years.

2. One thing that separates great leaders from good leaders is the way they invest in those who follow them. Just as you need a growth plan to improve, so do those who work for you. You can take groups of employees through books, bring in trainers, mentor people one on one—anything that works. Just make providing opportunities for growth your responsibility.

3. If you are the leader of a business, an organization, or a department, you can create a culture of growth. When people in your sphere of influence know that personal growth and leadership development are valued, resourced, and rewarded, then growth will explode. And the environment you created will begin attracting high achievers and people with great potential.

TAKE ACTION

While it is true that some people are born with greater natural gifts than others, the ability to lead is really a collection of skills, nearly all of which can be learned and improved. But that process doesn't happen overnight. Leadership is complicated. It has so many facets: respect, experience, emotional strength, people skills, discipline, vision, momentum, timing—the list goes on and on. As you can see, many of the factors that come into play in leadership are intangible. That's why leaders require so much seasoning to be effective.

This week, research or interview the person you admire as a leader in your profession or area of service. Ask that person the following questions.

1. What made you decide to enter the field in which you are successful?
2. Who were some of your mentors?
3. What five books have made the greatest impact on your leadership?
4. What daily learning or self-improvement habits do you have?

Ask yourself: What are the three most valuable things I have learned from this person's life, which I will apply to my own leadership growth?

Start reading one of the five books recommended to you.

4

THE LAW OF NAVIGATION

Anyone Can Steer the Ship, but
It Takes a Leader to Chart the Course

LEROY EIMS, AUTHOR OF *BE THE LEADER YOU WERE MEANT TO BE,* WRITES, "A leader is one who sees more than others see, who sees farther than others see, and who sees before others do." In order to be a successful leader, you must learn the importance of The Law of Navigation and be willing to navigate the course for your followers.

READ

In 1911, two groups of explorers set off on an incredible mission. Though they used different strategies and routes, the leaders of the teams had the same goal: to be the first in history to reach the South Pole. Their stories are life-and-death illustrations of the Law of Navigation.

One group was led by Norwegian explorer Roald Amundsen. Ironically, Amundsen had not originally intended to go to Antarctica. His desire was to be the first man to reach the *North* Pole. But when he discovered that Robert Peary had beaten him there, Amundsen changed his goal and headed toward the other end of the earth. North or south—he knew his planning would pay off.

Before his team ever set off, Amundsen had painstakingly planned his trip. He studied the methods of the Eskimos and other experienced Arctic travelers and determined that their best course of action would be to transport all their equipment and supplies by dogsled. When he assembled his team, he chose expert skiers and dog handlers. His strategy was simple. The dogs would do most of the work as the group traveled fifteen to twenty miles in a six-hour period each day. That would afford both the dogs and the men plenty of time for daily rest prior to the following day's travel.

Amundsen's forethought and attention to detail were incredible. He located and stocked supply depots all along the intended route. That way they would not have to carry every bit of their supplies with them the whole trip. He also equipped his people with the best gear possible. Amundsen had carefully considered every possible aspect of the journey, thought it through, and planned accordingly. And it paid off. The worst problem they experienced on their trip was an infected tooth that one man had to have extracted.

The other team of people was led by Robert Falcon Scott, a British naval officer who had previously done some exploring in the Antarctic area. Scott's expedition was the antithesis of Amundsen's. Instead of using dogsleds, Scott decided to use motorized sledges and ponies. Their problems began when the motors on the sledges stopped working only five days into the trip. The ponies didn't fare well either in those frigid temperatures. When they reached the foot of the Transantarctic Mountains, all of the poor animals had to be killed. As a result, the team members themselves ended up hauling the two-hundred-pound sledges. It was arduous work.

Scott hadn't given enough attention to the team's other equipment either. Their clothes were so poorly designed that all of the men developed frostbite. One team member required an hour every morning just to get his boots onto his swollen, gangrenous feet. Everyone became snowblind because of the inadequate goggles Scott had supplied. On top of everything else, the team was always low on food and water. That was also due to Scott's poor planning. The depots of supplies Scott established were inadequately stocked, too far apart, and often poorly marked, which made them very difficult to find. Because they were continually low on fuel to melt snow, everyone became dehydrated. Making things even worse was Scott's last-minute decision to take along a fifth man, even though they had prepared enough supplies for only four.

After covering a grueling eight hundred miles in ten weeks, Scott's exhausted group finally arrived at the South Pole on January 17, 1912. There they found the Norwegian flag flapping in the wind and a letter from Amundsen. The other well-led team had beaten them to their goal by more than a month!

Scott's expedition to the Pole is a classic example of a leader who could not navigate for his people. But the trek back was even worse. Scott and his men were starving and suffering from scurvy, yet Scott, unable to navigate to the very end, was oblivious to their plight. With time running out and the food supply desperately low, Scott insisted that they collect thirty pounds of geological specimens to take back—more weight to be carried by the worn-out men.

The group's progress became slower and slower. One member of the party sank into a stupor and died. Another, Lawrence Oates, a former army officer who had originally been brought along to take care of the ponies, had frostbite so severe that he had trouble doing anything. Because he believed he was endangering the team's survival, he purposely walked out into a blizzard to keep from hindering the group. Before he left the tent and headed into the storm, he said, "I am just going outside; I may be some time."

Scott and his final two team members made it only a little farther north before giving up. The return trip had already taken two months, and still they were 150 miles from their base camp. There they died. We know their story only because they spent their last hours updating their diaries. Some of Scott's last words were these: "We shall die like gentlemen. I think this will show that the Spirit of pluck and power to endure has not passed out of our race."[1] Scott had courage, but not leadership. Because he was unable to live by the Law of Navigation, he and his companions died by it.

OBSERVE

Followers need leaders able to effectively navigate for them. When they're facing life-and-death situations, the necessity is painfully obvious. But even when consequences aren't as serious, the need is also great. The truth is that nearly anyone can steer the ship, but it takes a leader to chart the course.

1. *What are some of the things that Amundsen planned for that Scott overlooked?*

_____

_____

_____

2. *How did Scott's lack of leadership skills affect his team?*

_____

_____

_____

3. *In your organization what events or projects could have been planned better? What do you think the outcome would have been if the team had a leader who was a good navigator?*

_____

_____

_____

4. *Who are the top navigators in your field? How have their leadership skills benefited their organizations?*

_____

_____

_____

LEARN

First-rate navigators always have in mind that other people are depending on them and their ability to chart a good course. I read an observation by James A. Autry in Life and Work: A Manager's Search for Meaning that illustrates this idea. He writes that occasionally you hear about the crash of four military planes flying together in a formation. The reason for the loss of all four is this: when jet fighters fly in groups of four, one pilot—the leader—designates where the team will fly. The other three planes fly on the leader's wing, watching him and following him wherever he goes. Whatever moves he makes, the rest of his team will make along with him. That's true whether he soars in the clouds or smashes into a mountaintop.

Before good leaders take their people on a journey, they go through a process in order to give the trip the best chance of being a success:

NAVIGATORS DRAW ON PAST EXPERIENCE

Every past success and failure you've experienced can be a valuable source of information and wisdom—if you allow it to be. Successes teach you what you're capable of doing and give you confidence. However, your failures often teach greater lessons. They reveal wrong assumptions, character flaws, errors in judgment, and poor working methods. Ironically, many people hate their failures so much that they quickly cover them up instead of analyzing them and learning from them. As I explain in my book *Failing Forward*, if you fail to learn from your mistakes, you're going to fail again and again.

Why do I even mention something that seems so basic? Because most natural leaders are activists. They tend to look forward—not backward—make decisions, and move on. I know this because that is my tendency. But for leaders to become good navigators, they need to take time to reflect and learn from their experiences. That's why I have developed the discipline of reflective thinking. I write about it in detail in my book *Thinking for a Change*, but allow me to give you some advantages of reflective thinking here. Reflective thinking . . .

gives you true perspective.
gives emotional integrity to your thought life.
increases your confidence in decision making.
clarifies the big picture.
takes a good experience and makes it a valuable experience.[2]

Each benefit gives a leader a great advantage when planning next steps for a team or organization.

NAVIGATORS EXAMINE THE CONDITIONS BEFORE MAKING COMMITMENTS

Drawing on experience means looking inward. Examining conditions means looking outward. No good leader plans a course of action without paying close attention to current conditions. That would be like setting sail against the tide or plotting a course into a hurricane. Good navigators count the cost *before* making commitments for themselves and others. They examine not only measurable factors such as finances, resources, and talent, but also intangibles such as timing, morale, momentum, culture, and so on. (I'll discuss this more in the Laws of Intuition and Timing.)

Navigators Listen to What Others Have to Say

No matter how much you learn from the past, it will never tell you all that you need to know for the present. No matter how good a leader you are, you yourself will not have all the answers. That's why top-notch navigators gather information from many sources. For example, before Roald Amundsen's expedition to the South Pole, he had learned from a group of Native Americans in Canada about warm clothing and Arctic survival techniques. Those skills and practices meant the difference between failure and success for his team in Antarctica.

Navigating leaders get ideas from many sources. They listen to members of their leadership team. They talk to the people in their organization to find out what's happening on the grassroots level. And they spend time with leaders from outside the organization who can mentor them. They always think in terms of relying on a team, not just themselves.

Navigators Make Sure Their Conclusions Represent Both Faith and Fact

Being able to navigate for others requires a leader to possess a positive attitude. You've got to have faith that you can take your people all the way. If you can't confidently make the trip in your mind, you're not going to be able to take it in real life.

On the other hand, you also have to be able to see the facts realistically. You can't minimize obstacles or rationalize your challenges and still lead effectively. If you don't go in with your eyes wide open, you're going to get blindsided. As Bill Easum, president of Easum, Bandy, and Associates, observes, "Realistic leaders are objective enough to minimize illusions. They understand that self-deception can cost them their vision."

Jim Collins confirmed this balance between faith and fact in his 2001 book *Good to Great*. He calls it the Stockdale Paradox. He writes, "You must retain faith that you will prevail in the end *and* you must also confront the most brutal facts of your current reality."[3] Balancing optimism and realism, intuition and planning, faith and fact can be very difficult. But that's what it takes to be effective as a navigating leader.

DISCUSS

Answer the following questions and discuss your answers when you meet with your team.

1. *What is the process you should go through in order to successfully navigate your team?*

    _____

    _____

    _____

2. *Do you agree that all four steps in the navigation process are necessary? Explain.*

    _____

    _____

    _____

3. *Which step in the navigation process do you find most difficult? Why?*

    _____

    _____

    _____

4. *How do you choose who to run your ideas by before implementing them?*

    _____

    _____

    _____

5. *Describe a situation in which you skipped one of the steps in the navigation process. What was the outcome?*

    _____

    _____

    _____

6. *How do you prepare your team for projects? In your opinion do you need to spend more time on planning? What prevents you from doing so? How can you more effectively plan to plan?*

_____

_____

_____

APPLY

1. Do you make it a regular practice to reflect on your positive and negative experiences? If not, you will miss the potential lessons they have to offer. Do one of two things. Set aside a time to reflect every week, examining your calendar or journal to jog your memory. Or build reflection time into your schedule, so that it's immediately available after every major success or failure. In either case, write down what you learn during that discovery process.

2. Navigating leaders do their homework. For some project or major task that you are currently responsible for, draw on your past experience, hold intentional conversations with experts and team members to gather information, and examine current conditions that could impact the success of your endeavor. Only after taking these steps should you create your action plan.

3. Which way do you naturally lean—toward facts or faith? Rarely is a leader especially talented in both areas. (I'm a faith person. I am highly visionary and believe that anything is possible. I often rely on my brother, Larry, to help me with realistic thinking.) Yet good navigators must be able to do both.

To successfully practice the Law of Navigation, you must know your own bent. If you're not sure, ask trusted friends and colleagues. Then make sure you have someone with the opposite bent on your team so that you can work together.

TAKE ACTION

Use the following acrostic to plan and execute an upcoming project with your team. Follow the example given.

EXAMPLE PROJECT: COMPANY GROWTH

Predetermine a Course of Action

    In order to grow we need a new facility.

Lay out Your Goals

    Our goals are: design and build the facility, pay for it in ten years, keep morale high in the process.

Adjust Your Priorities

    Our priority is: to have a solid financial plan so the business isn't strained during building.

Notify Key Personnel

    The people who need to know about the plan are people with the most influence, key leaders, people working on the project.

Allow Time for Acceptance

    We will announce the project in two-hour presentations to the board and follow up three days later.

Head into Action

    The first step for building the new facility is zoning.

Expect Problems

    A roadblock to our progress may be zoning issues. We will plan for this roadblock by researching the zoning laws in our county.

Always Point to Success

    We will give success updates by sending out a memo every other Monday morning.

Daily Review Your Planning

    The project leaders will communicate each day by holding a fifteen-minute meeting each morning.

5

THE LAW OF ADDITION

Leaders Add Value by Serving Others

MANY PEOPLE VIEW LEADERSHIP THE SAME WAY THEY VIEW SUCCESS, hoping to go as far as they can, to climb the ladder, to achieve the highest position possible for their talent. But contrary to conventional thinking, I believe the bottom line in leadership isn't how far we advance ourselves, but how far we advance others. That is achieved by serving others and adding value to their lives.

READ

In a world where many political leaders enjoy their power and prestige and where CEOs of large corporations make astronomical incomes, work and live in luxury, and appear to be most concerned with what's in it for them, Jim Sinegal is an oddity.

Sinegal is the cofounder and CEO of Costco, the fourth largest retailer in the U.S. and the ninth largest in the world. He doesn't seem much interested in perks. He works in an unremarkable office comprised primarily of folding tables and chairs. If he invites someone to meet him at the corporate offices, he goes down to the lobby to meet his guest. He answers his own phone. And he takes a salary of only $350,000 a year, which puts him in the bottom 10 percent of CEOs of large corporations.

Sinegal's path to corporate leadership wasn't typical either. He didn't attend an Ivy League school. He isn't a lawyer or a CPA. As a teenager, he thought of becoming a doctor, but his high school grades were less than stellar. So he went off to community college and earned an associate's degree. While he was attending San Diego State College (now University), he helped a friend unload mattresses at a new local retail store called Fed-Mart. That one day of work turned into a regular job. When he received a promotion, he discontinued his studies. He had found his career. In time, he had also found a mentor, Sol Price, Fed-Mart's chairman. Under Price's guidance, Sinegal rose to the post of executive vice president for merchandising. Sinegal later helped Price found Price Club, then went on to cofound Costco in 1983 with Jeffrey H. Brotman. The company's growth was rapid. Costco purchased and merged with Price Club ten years later.

Retail experts give a lot of attention to Sinegal's formula for success: offer a limited number of items, rely on high volume sales, keep costs as low as possible, and don't spend money on advertising. But there is something that separates him from the competitors who employ similar strategies: the way he treats his employees. He believes in paying his employees well and offering them good benefit packages. Costco employees are paid an average of 42 percent more than the company's chief rival. And Costco employees pay a fraction of the national average for health care. Sinegal believes that if you pay people well, "You get good people and good productivity."[1] You also get employee loyalty. Costco has by far the lowest employee turnover rate in all of retailing.

But Sinegal's leadership style of adding value doesn't end with employee compensation. He goes out of his way to show Costco workers that he cares about them. He maintains an open-door policy with everyone. He wears an employee name tag, is on a first-name basis with everyone, and makes sure to visit every single Costco store at least once a year.

"No manager and no staff in any business feels very good if the boss is not interested enough to come and see them," says Sinegal. And when he shows up, his people are always glad to seem him. "The employees know that I want to say hello to them, because I like them."[2]

Sinegal goes out of his way to show his people that he cares. He once flew from Texas to the San Francisco area when he heard that a Costco executive was hospitalized for emergency surgery. It came as no surprise to the executive. It was consistent with the way Sinegal always leads.

Sol Price, Sinegal's one-time mentor, says, "Jim has done a very good job in balancing the interests of the shareholders, the employees, the customers and the managers. Most companies tilt too much one way or another." Many of the lessons Sinegal learned came from Price, who believed in treating people well and giving them credit. In a meeting at Fed-Mart, Sinegal noted that a manager was quick to take the credit and to place blame on others. But Price saw through him.

"To teach us all a lesson," recalls Sinegal, "Sol used a weekly meeting to purposely raise hell about something that was wrong in one of the stores. I wondered why he did it. But when he saw that this manager let two of his employees take the blame, he fired him within a week.

"It's improper for one person to take credit when it takes so many people to build a successful organization," asserts Sinegal. "When you try to be top dog, you don't create loyalty. If you can't give credit (and take blame), you will drown in your inability to inspire."[3]

The only real criticism of Sinegal comes from Wall Street. Analysts there believe that Sinegal is too kind and generous to his people. They would like to see him pay employees less and squeeze them more. But Sinegal wouldn't think of it. He believes that if you treat the employees and customers right, profits will follow. "On Wall Street," he observes, "they're in the business of making money between now and next Thursday. I don't say that with any bitterness, but we can't take that view. We want to build a company that will still be here 50 and 60 years from now."[4]

Others outside the organization appreciate his approach to business. Nell Minow, an expert on corporate governance, remarked, "I would love to clone him. Of the 2,000 companies in our database, he has the single shortest CEO employment contract." It's less than a page long. "And [it's] the only one which specifically says he can be—believe it or not—'terminated for cause.'"[5]

When it comes down to it, Sinegal is more focused on adding value to people by serving them than on serving himself or making himself richer with an exorbitant salary. He lives by the Law of Addition. "I just think that if you're going to try to run an organization that's very cost-conscious, then you can't have those disparities. Having an individual who is making 100 or 200 or 300 times more than the average person working on the floor is wrong."[6]

Sinegal sums it up this way: "This is not altruistic. This is good business." He could also say it's good leadership!

OBSERVE

The interaction between every leader and follower is a relationship, and all relationships either add to or subtract from a person's life. If you are a leader, then trust me, you are having either a positive or a negative impact on the people you lead.

1. *How did Sinegal add value to the employees of Costco?*

   _____

   _____

   _____

2. *What is Sinegal's return on his investment in his employees?*

   _____

   _____

   _____

3. *Why should leaders lead? And when they do, what is their first responsibility?*

   _____

   _____

   _____

4. *Does a leader's motive matter, or is it simply getting the job done that's important? What's the bottom line?*

   _____

   _____

   _____

5. *How do you respond differently to a leader who serves self verses a leader who serves the team?*

_____

_____

_____

LEARN

I have developed four guidelines to help me add value to others. Three of them are fundamental and can be used by anyone desiring to practice the Law of Addition. The fourth is based on my faith. If that might offend you or you don't have interest in that area, then simply skip it.

1. We Add Value to Others When We . . . Truly Value Others

Darryl Hartley-Leonard, who retired as chairman of the board of Hyatt Hotels Corporation and is currently chairman and chief executive officer of Production Group International, says, "When a person moves into a position of authority, he or she gives up the right to abuse people." I believe that is true. But that is only the beginning of good leadership. Effective leaders go beyond not harming others, and they intentionally help others. To do that, they must value people and demonstrate that they care in such a way that their followers know it.

Dan Reiland, who was my right-hand man for many years, is an excellent leader and values people highly. But when he first came to work for me, he didn't show it. One day when he was new on the job, I was chatting with some people in the lobby, and Dan came in, briefcase in hand. Dan walked right past all of us without saying a word and went straight down the hall toward his office. I was astounded. How could a leader walk right by a group of people he worked with and not even say hello to them? I quickly excused myself from the conversation I was having and followed Dan to his office.

"Dan," I asked after greeting him, "how could you walk right past everybody like that?"

"I've got a lot of work to do today," Dan answered, "and really want to get started."

"Dan," I said, "you just walked past your work. Never forget that leadership is about people." Dan cared about people and wanted to serve them as a leader. He just didn't show it.

I'm told that in American Sign Language, the sign for serving is to hold the hands out in front with the palms up and to move them back and forth between the signer and the signee. And really, that is a good metaphor for the attitude that servant leaders should possess: they should be open, trusting, caring, offering their help, and willing to be vulnerable. Leaders who add value by serving believe in their people before their people believe in them and serve others before they are served.

2. We Add Value to Others When We . . . Make Ourselves More Valuable to Others

The whole idea of adding value to other people depends on the idea that you have something of value to add. You can't give what you do not possess. If you have skills, you gained them through study and practice. If you have opportunities to give, you acquired them through hard work. If you possess wisdom, you gained it by intentionally evaluating the experiences you've had. The more intentional you have been in growing personally, the more you have to offer. The more you continue to pursue personal growth, the more you will continue to have to offer.

3. We Add Value to Others When We . . . Know and Relate to What Others Value

Management consultant Nancy K. Austin says that once when she looked under the bed in her room at one of her favorite hotels, she was surprised to find a card. It said, "Yes, we clean under here too!" "I don't remember the lobby, or the number of chandeliers, or how many square feet of marble they cobbled together to make our underfoot experience pleasant." What she remembered was that card. The housekeeping staff had anticipated what was important to her and had served her well.

We think of that as good customer service, and when we are clients or guests, we expect to receive it. But as leaders, we don't automatically expect to give it. But it is a key to effective leadership. As leaders, how do we know and relate to what our people value? We listen.

Inexperienced leaders are quick to lead before knowing anything about the people they intend to lead. But mature leaders listen, learn, and then lead. They *listen* to their people's stories. They find out about their hopes and dreams. They become acquainted with their aspirations. And they pay attention to their emotions. From those things, they *learn* about their people. They discover what is valuable to them. And *then* they *lead* based upon what they've learned. When they do that, everybody wins—the organization, the leader, and the followers.

4. WE ADD VALUE TO OTHERS WHEN WE . . . DO THINGS THAT GOD VALUES

I already mentioned that you may want to skip this final point, but for me it's a non-negotiable. I believe that God desires us not only to treat people with respect, but also to actively reach out to them and serve them. Scripture provides many examples and descriptions of how we should conduct ourselves, but here is my favorite, captured by Eugene Peterson's *The Message*:

When he finally arrives, blazing in beauty and all his angels with him, the Son of Man will take his place on his glorious throne. Then all the nations will be arranged before him and he will sort the people out, much as a shepherd sorts out sheep and goats, putting sheep to his right and goats to his left.

Then the King will say to those on his right, "Enter, you who are blessed by my Father! Take what's coming to you in this kingdom. It's been ready for you since the world's foundation. And here's why:

I was hungry and you fed me,
I was thirsty and you gave me a drink,
I was homeless and you gave me a room,
I was shivering and you gave me clothes,
I was sick and you stopped to visit,
I was in prison and you came to me."

Then those "sheep" are going to say, "Master, what are you talking about? When did we ever see you hungry and feed you, thirsty and give you a drink? And when did we ever see you sick or in prison and come to you?" Then the King will say, "I'm telling the solemn truth: Whenever you did one of these things to someone overlooked or ignored, that was me—you did it to me."[7]

That standard for my conduct influences everything I do, not just including my leadership, but especially my leadership. Because the more power I have, the greater my impact on others—for better or worse. And I always want to be someone who adds value to others, not takes it away.

DISCUSS

Answer the following questions and discuss your answers when you meet with your team.

1. *What does it mean to "add value" to someone?*

    _____

    _____

    _____

2. *Describe how someone has added value to you.*

    _____

    _____

    _____

3. *What evidence can you point to that supports the positive influence you've had on someone you led?*

    _____

    _____

    _____

4. *What steps have you taken—or will you take—to understand what the people on your team value?*

_____

_____

_____

5. *How can your own personal growth help you to better serve the people on your team?*

_____

_____

_____

APPLY

1. Do you have a servant's attitude when it comes to leadership? Don't be too quick to say yes. Here's how you can tell. In situations where you are required to serve others' needs, how do you respond? Do you become impatient? Do you feel resentful? Do you believe that certain tasks are beneath your dignity or position? If you answer yes to any of those questions, then your attitude is not as good as it could be. Make it a practice to perform small acts of service for others without seeking credit or recognition for them. Continue until you no longer resent doing them.

2. What do the people closest to you value? Make a list of the most important people in your life—from home, work, church, hobbies, and so on. After making the list, write what each person values most. Then rate yourself on a scale of 1 (poorly) to 10 (excellently) on how well you relate to that person's values. If you can't articulate what someone values or you score lower than an 8 in relating to that person, spend more time with him or her to improve

3. Make adding value part of your lifestyle. Begin with those closest to you. How could you add value to the people on your list related to what *they* value? Start doing it. Then do the same with all the people you lead. If there are only a few, add value individually. If you lead large numbers of people, you may have to think of ways to serve groups as well as individuals.

TAKE ACTION

What do you have to give others? Can you teach skills? Can you give opportunities? Can you give insight and perspective gained through experience? You can add value to someone.

List below the name of the person you will add value to over the next few months, and fill in the related phrase. Then set up a consistent time to meet with this person over the next few months.

I will mentor:

_____

Why I chose this person:

_____

_____

What I have to offer this person:

_____

_____

Three ways I can add to this person's life:

1. _____

_____

2. _____

_____

3. _____

_____

We will meet (once each / every other) week for _____ months.

6

THE LAW OF SOLID GROUND

Trust Is the Foundation of Leadership

How important is trust for a leader? It is *the most important* thing. Trust is the foundation of leadership. It is the glue that holds an organization together. Leaders cannot repeatedly break trust with people and continue to influence them. It just doesn't happen.

READ

Watergate and other various public scandals have undermined the public's confidence in America's leaders during the last thirty years. But the event that I believe began to erode the public's faith in the nation's leaders and developed strong skepticism in the country was the war in Vietnam. The actions taken by members of the Johnson administration, the mistakes made by Robert McNamara, and their unwillingness to face and admit those mistakes broke trust with the American people. They violated the Law of Solid Ground, and the United States has been suffering from the repercussions ever since.

Vietnam was already at war when President Kennedy and Robert McNamara, his secretary of defense, took office in January of 1961. The Vietnam region had been a battleground for decades, and the United States got involved in the mid-1950s when President Eisenhower sent a small number of U.S. troops to Vietnam as advisors. When Kennedy took office, he continued Eisenhower's policy. It was always his intention to let the South Vietnamese fight and win their own war, but over time, the United

States became increasingly involved. Before the war was over, more than half a million American troops at a time served in Vietnam.

If you experienced those war years, you may be surprised to know that in the beginning American support for the war was very strong, even as the number of troops being sent overseas rapidly increased and the casualties mounted. By 1966, more than two hundred thousand Americans had been sent to Vietnam, yet two-thirds of all Americans surveyed by Louis Harris believed that Vietnam was the place where the United States should "stand and fight communism." And most people expressed the belief that the U.S. should stay until the fight was finished.

But support eventually eroded. The Vietnam War was being handled very badly. On top of that, our leaders continued the war even after they realized that we couldn't win it. But the worst mistake of all was that McNamara and President Johnson weren't honest with the American people about it. And because trust is the foundation of leadership, it ultimately destroyed the administration's leadership.

In his book *In Retrospect,* McNamara recounts that he repeatedly minimized American losses and told only half-truths about the war. For example, he says, "Upon my return to Washington [from Saigon] on December 21, [1963] I was less than candid when I reported to the press . . . I said, 'We observed the results of a very substantial increase in Vietcong activity' (true); but I then added, 'We reviewed the plans of the South Vietnamese and we have every reason to believe they will be successful' (an overstatement at best)."

For a while, nobody questioned McNamara's statements because there was no reason to mistrust the country's leaders. But in time, people recognized that his words and the facts weren't matching up. And that's when the American public began to lose faith. Years later, McNamara admitted his failure: "We of the Kennedy and Johnson administrations who participated in the decisions on Vietnam acted according to what we thought were the principles and traditions of this nation. We made our decisions in light of those values. Yet we were wrong, terribly wrong."[1]

Many would argue that McNamara's admission came thirty years and fifty-eight thousand lives too late. The cost of Vietnam was high, and not just in human lives. As the American people's trust in their leaders deteriorated, so did their willingness to follow them. Protests led to open rebellion and to society-wide turmoil. The era that had begun with the hope and idealism characterized by John F. Kennedy ultimately ended with the mistrust and cynicism associated with Richard Nixon.

Whenever a leader breaks the Law of Solid Ground, he pays a price in his leadership. McNamara and President Johnson lost the trust of the American people, and their ability to lead suffered as a result. Eventually, McNamara resigned as secretary of defense. Johnson, the consummate politician, recognized his weakened position, and he didn't run for reelection. But the repercussions of broken trust didn't end there. The American people's distrust for politicians has continued to this day.

No leader can break trust with his people and expect to keep influencing them. Trust is the foundation of leadership. Violate the Law of Solid Ground, and you diminish your influence as a leader.

OBSERVE

Craig Weatherup, who retired as founding chairman and CEO of the Pepsi Bottling Group, acknowledges, "People will tolerate honest mistakes, but if you violate their trust you will find it very difficult to ever regain their confidence. That is one reason that you need to treat trust as your most precious asset. You may fool your boss but you can never fool your colleagues or subordinates."

1. *How did Robert McNamara violate the trust of the American people?*

_____

_____

_____

2. *How did McNamara and Johnson's actions reflect on the rest of the American government?*

_____

_____

_____

3. *Give an example of a time when a leader violated your trust. What was your reaction?*

_____

_____

_____

4. *After your trust has been violated, how is it regained?*

_____

_____

_____

5 *Can you think of instances in which you have violated followers' trust? If so, how will you work to restore it?*

_____

_____

_____

LEARN

Trust is the foundation of leadership. How does a leader build trust? By consistently exemplifying competence, connection, and character. People will forgive occasional mistakes based on ability, especially if they can see that you're still growing as a leader. And they will give you some time to connect. But they won't trust someone who has slips in character. In that area, even occasional lapses are lethal. All effective leaders know this truth.

General H. Norman Schwarzkopf points to the significance of character: "Leadership is a potent combination of strategy and character. But if you must be without one, be without strategy." Character and leadership credibility always go hand in hand. Anthony Harrigan, president of the U.S. Business and Industrial Council, said,

The role of character always has been the key factor in the rise and fall of nations. And one can be sure that America is no exception to this rule of history. We won't survive as a country because we are smarter or more sophisticated but because we are—we hope—stronger inwardly. In short, character is the only effective bulwark against internal and external forces that lead to a country's disintegration or collapse.

Character makes trust possible. And trust makes leadership possible. Whenever you lead people, it's as if they consent to take a journey with you. The way that trip is going to turn out is predicted by your character. With good character, the longer the trip is, the better it seems. But if your character is flawed, the longer the trip is, the worse it gets. Why? Because no one enjoys spending time with someone he doesn't trust.

A person's character quickly communicates many things to others. Here are the most important ones:

CHARACTER COMMUNICATES CONSISTENCY

Leaders without inner strength can't be counted on day after day because their ability to perform changes constantly. NBA great Jerry West commented, "You can't get too much done in life if you only work on the days when you feel good." If your people don't know what to expect from you as a leader, at some point they won't look to you for leadership.

When I think of leaders who epitomize consistency of character, the first person who comes to mind is Billy Graham. Regardless of personal religious beliefs, everybody trusts him. Why? Because he has modeled high character for more than half a century. He lives out his values every day. He never makes a commitment unless he is going to keep it. And he goes out of his way to personify integrity.

CHARACTER COMMUNICATES POTENTIAL

British politician and writer John Morley observed, "No man can climb out beyond the limitations of his own character." Weak character is limiting. Who do you think has the greater potential to achieve great dreams and have a positive impact on others: someone who is honest, disciplined, and hardworking, or someone who is deceitful, impulsive, and lazy? It sounds obvious when it's phrased that way, doesn't it?

Talent alone is never enough. It must be bolstered by character if a person desires to go far. Think about someone like the NFL's Terrell Owens. Few football players have his talent. Yet he seems unable to get along with his teammates, wherever he plays. If he keeps going on the same track, he will never fulfill his potential as a player.

Poor character is like a time bomb ticking away. It's only a matter of time before it blows up a person's ability to perform and the capacity to lead. Why? Because people with weak character are not trustworthy, and trust is the foundation of leadership. Craig Weatherup explains, "You don't build trust by talking about it. You build it by achieving results, always with integrity and in a manner that shows real personal regard for the people with whom you work."[2]

When a leader's character is strong, people trust him, and they trust in his ability to release their potential. That not only gives his followers hope for the future, but it also promotes a strong belief in themselves and their organization.

Character Communicates Respect

When you don't have character within, you can't earn respect without. And respect is absolutely essential for lasting leadership. How do leaders earn respect? By making sound decisions, by admitting their mistakes, and by putting what's best for their followers and the organization ahead of their personal agendas.

Years ago a movie was made about the Fifty-fourth Massachusetts Infantry regiment and its colonel, Robert Gould Shaw. The film was called *Glory,* and though some of its plot was fictionalized, the Civil War story of Shaw's journey with his men—and of the respect he earned from them—was real.

The movie recounted the formation of this unit in the Union army, which was the first to be composed of African-American soldiers. Shaw, a white officer, took command of the regiment, oversaw recruiting, selected the (white) officers, equipped the men, and trained them as soldiers. He drove them hard, knowing that their performance in battle would either vindicate or condemn the value of black people as soldiers and citizens in the minds of many white Northerners. In the process, the soldiers and Shaw earned one another's respect.

A few months after their training was complete, the men of the Fifty-fourth got the opportunity to prove themselves in the Union assault on Confederate Fort Wagner in South Carolina. Shaw's biographer Russell Duncan said of the attack: "With a final admonition to 'prove yourselves men,' Shaw positioned himself in front and ordered, 'forward.' Years later, one soldier remembered that the regiment fought hard because Shaw was in front, not behind."

Almost half of the six hundred men from the Fifty-fourth who fought that day were wounded, captured, or killed. Though they fought valiantly, they were unable to take Fort Wagner. And Shaw, who had courageously led his men to the top of the fort's parapet in the first assault, was killed alongside his men.

Shaw's actions on that final day solidified the respect his men already had for him. Two weeks after the battle, Albanus Fisher, a sergeant in the Fifty-fourth, said, "I still feel more Eager for the struggle than I ever yet have, for I now wish to have Revenge for our galant Curnel [*sic*]."[3] J. R. Miller once observed, "The only thing that walks back from the tomb with the mourners and refuses to be buried is the character of a man. This is true. What a man is survives him. It can never be buried." Shaw's character, strong to the last, had communicated a level of respect to his men that lived beyond him.

DISCUSS

Answer the following questions and discuss your answers when you meet with your team.

1. *Do you agree with the author that to build trust a leader must exemplify competence, connection and character? Can you gain trust without one of these characteristics? Is there another characteristic you would add? Explain.*

_____

_____

_____

2. *How effective will a leader be if he or she has lost the trust of the team?*

_____

_____

_____

3. *How does character communicate consistency, potential, and respect? Give an example for each.*

_____

_____

_____

4. *What is the quickest way for a person to lose your trust?*

_____

_____

_____

5. *How would you handle a situation in which you worked with someone you didn't trust?*

_____

_____

_____

6. *How do you gain and maintain the trust of others?*

_____

_____

_____

7. *Of the three trust-building factors — competence, connection, character — which is your strength? In which are you weakest? Why?*

_____

_____

_____

APPLY

1. How trustworthy would your followers say you are? How can you measure their trust? By how open they are with you. Do they openly share opinions with you—even negative ones? Do they give you bad news as readily as good news? Do they let you know what's going on in their areas of responsibility? If not, they may not trust your character.

How about your colleagues and your leader? Do they consistently put their trust in you?

How do you measure their trust? By how much responsibility they entrust to you. If you regularly carry weighty responsibilities, that is a good sign that you are trustworthy. If not, then you need to find out whether they doubt your competence or your character.

2. Most high achievers spend time developing their professional skills. They seek to be highly competent. Fewer focus on their character. What are you currently doing to develop your character?

I recommend that you focus on three main areas: integrity, authenticity, and discipline. To develop your integrity, make a commitment to yourself to be scrupulously honest. Don't shave the truth, don't tell white lies, and don't fudge numbers. Be truthful even when it hurts. To develop authenticity, be yourself with everyone. Don't play politics, role play, or pretend to be anything you're not. To strengthen your discipline, do the right things every day regardless of how you feel.

3. If you have broken trust with others in the past, then your leadership will always suffer until you try to make things right. First, apologize to whomever you have hurt or betrayed. If you can make amends or restitution, then do so. And commit to work at re-earning their trust. The greater the violation, the longer it will take. The onus is not on them to trust. The onus is on you to earn it. (And if you have broken trust at home, start there before working to repair professional relationships.)

TAKE ACTION

When you work with others you have a number of opportunities to display your competence, connection, and character in the decisions you make and actions you take. With every decision and action, you are either gaining or losing change, building or losing trust.

Take time to evaluate your current level of trust with the team you are leading or working with now.

1. *Overall, how would your team rate your competence—high or low?*

   _____

2. *Have there been times when mistakes you made held the team back? If so, how do you think it has damaged people's trust in you? How can you repair it?*

   _____

   _____

   _____

3. *List the names of the people on your team. Next to each name, give an example of how you have made an effort to connect with that person.*

Name: Connection:

_____   _____

_____   _____

_____   _____

_____   _____

_____   _____

_____   _____

_____   _____

4. *How does your level of connection affect your ability to lead or work with the people you listed? Who should you spend more time connecting with? How do you plan to do this?*

_____

_____

_____

5. *Give yourself a grade on a scale of 1-10 (one being an area of weakness and 10 being an area of strength) on each of the following character areas:*

Commitment	1 2 3 4 5 6 7 8 9 10
Courage	1 2 3 4 5 6 7 8 9 10
Honesty	1 2 3 4 5 6 7 8 9 10
Perseverance	1 2 3 4 5 6 7 8 9 10
Preparedness	1 2 3 4 5 6 7 8 9 10
Respect for others	1 2 3 4 5 6 7 8 9 10
Responsibility	1 2 3 4 5 6 7 8 9 10
Self-discipline	1 2 3 4 5 6 7 8 9 10
Teachability	1 2 3 4 5 6 7 8 9 10
Unselfishness	1 2 3 4 5 6 7 8 9 10

6. *To better evaluate your character, talk to someone in your work environment whom you trust and who can honestly give you feedback about what areas of your character or how you express yourself you can work on.*

_____

_____

_____

7

THE LAW OF RESPECT

People Naturally Follow Leaders Stronger Than Themselves

WHEN PEOPLE RESPECT A PERSON, THEY ADMIRE HER. WHEN THEY RESPECT her as a friend, they love her. When respect her as a leader, they follow her. There are different forms and levels of respect, and if you want to influence others you need to be respected as a leader. And in order to do that, you will have to prove yourself and your abilities as stated by the *Law of Respect*. As Clarence B. Randall said, "The leader must know, must know he knows, and must be able to make it abundantly clear to those around him that he knows."

READ

If you had seen her, your first reaction might not have been respect. She wasn't a very impressive-looking woman—just a little over five feet tall, in her late thirties, with dark brown weathered skin. She couldn't read or write. The clothes she wore were coarse and worn. When she smiled, she revealed that her top two front teeth were missing.

She lived alone. The story was that she had abandoned her husband when she was twenty-nine. She gave him no warning. One day he woke up, and she was gone. She talked to him only once after that, years later, and afterward she never mentioned his name again.

Her employment was erratic. Most of the time she took domestic jobs in small hotels: scrubbing floors, making up rooms, and cooking. But just about every spring and fall she would disappear from her place of employment, come back broke, and work again to scrape together what little money she could. When she was present on the job, she worked hard and seemed physically tough, but she also was known to suddenly fall asleep—sometimes in the middle of a conversation. She attributed her affliction to a blow to the head she had taken during a teenage fight.

Who would respect a woman like that? The answer is the more than three hundred slaves who followed her to freedom out of the South—they recognized and respected her leadership. So did just about every abolitionist in New England. The year was 1857. The woman's name was Harriet Tubman.

While she was only in her thirties, Harriet Tubman came to be called Moses because of her ability to go into the land of captivity and bring so many of her people out of slavery's bondage. Tubman started life as a slave. She was born in 1820 and grew up in the farmland of Maryland. When she was thirteen, she received the blow to her head that troubled her all her life. She was in a store, and a white overseer demanded her assistance so that he could beat an escaping slave. When she refused and blocked the overseer's way, the man threw a two-pound weight that hit Tubman in the head. She nearly died, and her recovery took months.

At age twenty-four, she married John Tubman, a free black man. But when she talked to him about escaping to freedom in the North, he wouldn't hear of it. He said that if she tried to leave, he'd turn her in. When she resolved to take her chances and go north in 1849, she did so alone, without a word to him. Her first biographer, Sarah Bradford, said that Tubman told her: "I had reasoned this out in my mind: there was one of two things I had a *right* to, liberty or death. If I could not have one, I would have the other, for no man should take me alive. I should fight for my liberty as my strength lasted, and when the time came for me to go, the Lord would let them take me."

Tubman made her way to Philadelphia, Pennsylvania, via the Underground Railroad, a secret network of free blacks, white abolitionists, and Quakers who helped escaping slaves on the run. Though free herself, she vowed to return to Maryland and bring her family out. In 1850, she made her first return trip as an Underground Railroad "conductor"—someone who retrieved and guided out slaves with the assistance of sympathizers along the way.

Each summer and winter, Tubman worked as a domestic, scraping together the funds she needed to make return trips to the South. And every spring and fall, she risked her life by going south and returning with more people. She was fearless, and her leadership was unshakable. Hers was extremely dangerous work, and when people in her charge wavered or had second thoughts, she was strong as steel. Tubman knew escaped slaves who returned would be beaten and tortured until they gave information about those who had helped them. So she never allowed any people she was guiding to give up. "Dead folks tell no tales," she would tell a fainthearted slave as she put a loaded pistol to his head. "You go on or die!"

Between 1850 and 1860, Harriet Tubman guided out more than three hundred people, including many of her family members. She made nineteen trips in all and was very proud of the fact that she never once lost a single person under her care. "I never ran my train off the track," she said, "and I never lost a passenger." At the time, Southern whites put a $12,000 price on her head—a fortune. Southern blacks simply called her Moses. By the start of the Civil War, she had brought more people out of slavery than any other American in history—black or white, male or female.

Tubman's reputation and influence commanded respect, and not just among slaves who dreamed of gaining their freedom. Influential Northerners of both races sought her out. She spoke at rallies and in homes throughout Philadelphia, Pennsylvania; Boston, Massachusetts; St. Catharines, Canada; and Auburn, New York, where she eventually settled. People of prominence sought her out, such as Senator William Seward, who later became Abraham Lincoln's secretary of state, and outspoken abolitionist and former slave Frederick Douglass. Tubman's advice and leadership were also requested by John Brown, the famed revolutionary abolitionist. Brown always referred to the former slave as "General Tubman," and he was quoted as saying she "was a better officer than most whom he had seen, and could command an army as successfully as she had led her small parties of fugitives."[1] That is the essence of the Law of Respect.

OBSERVE

Harriet Tubman would appear to be an unlikely candidate for leadership because the deck was certainly stacked against her. She was uneducated. She began life as a slave.

She lived in a culture that didn't respect African-Americans. And she labored in a country where women didn't have the right to vote yet. Despite her circumstances, she became an incredible leader. The reason is simple: people naturally follow leaders stronger than themselves. Everyone who came in contact with her recognized her strong leadership ability and felt compelled to follow her. That's how the *Law of Respect* works.

1. *Why wasn't Harriet Tubman an obvious choice as a leader?*

   _____

   _____

   _____

2. *How did Harriet Tubman gain respect?*

   _____

   _____

   _____

3. *How did respect factor into her leadership abilities?*

   _____

   _____

   _____

4. *Who is the person you respect the most in your profession? Why is this person so highly respected? What has this person been able to accomplish?*

   _____

   _____

   _____

5. *Who do you most respect in your organization? Why?*

   _____

   _____

   _____

LEARN

People don't follow others by accident. They follow individuals whose leadership they respect. People who are an 8 in leadership (on a scale from 1 to 10, with 10 being the strongest) don't go out and look for a 6 to follow—they naturally follow a 9 or 10. The less skilled follow the more highly skilled and gifted. Occasionally, a strong leader may choose to follow someone weaker than himself. But when that happens, it's for a reason. For example, the stronger leader may do it out of respect for the person's office or past accomplishments. Or he may be following the chain of command. In general, though, followers are attracted to people who are better leaders than themselves. That is the Law of Respect.

When people get together for the first time in a group, take a look at what happens. As they start interacting, the leaders in the group immediately take charge. They think in terms of the direction they desire to go and who they want to take with them. At first, people may make tentative moves in many different directions, but after the people get to know one another, it doesn't take long for them to recognize the strongest leaders and to start following them.

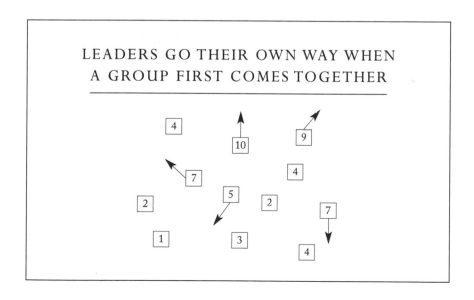

LEADERS GO THEIR OWN WAY WHEN
A GROUP FIRST COMES TOGETHER

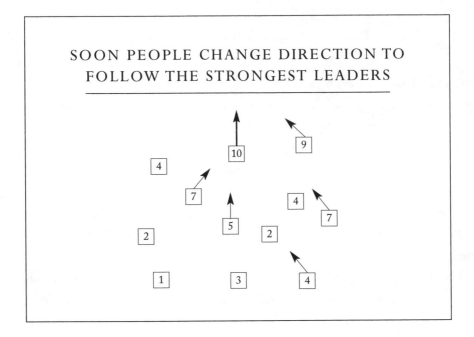

SOON PEOPLE CHANGE DIRECTION TO
FOLLOW THE STRONGEST LEADERS

PEOPLE NATURALLY ALIGN THEMSELVES
AND FOLLOW LEADERS
STRONGER THAN THEMSELVES

Usually the more leadership ability a person has, the more quickly he recognizes leadership—or its lack—in others. In time, people in the group get on board and follow the strongest leaders. Either that or they leave the group and pursue their own agenda.

I remember hearing a story that shows how people come to follow stronger leaders. It happened in the early 1970s when Hall of Fame basketball center Bill Walton joined Coach John Wooden's UCLA team. As a young man, Walton wore a beard. It has been said that the coach told Walton that UCLA players were not allowed to have facial hair. Walton, attempting to assert his independence, said that he would not shave off his beard. Wooden's no-nonsense response was, "We'll miss you, Bill." Needless to say, Walton shaved the beard.

What causes one person to respect and follow another? Is it because of the qualities of the leader? Is it due to a process the leader and follower engage in? Does it occur because of the circumstances? I believe all of those factors can come into play. Based on my observations and personal experience, here are the top six ways that leaders gain others' respect:

1. NATURAL LEADERSHIP ABILITY

First and foremost is leadership ability. Some people are born with greater skills and ability to lead than others. All leaders are not created equal. However, as I've stated in the Law of the Lid and the Law of Process, every person can become a better leader.

If you possess natural leadership ability, people will want to follow you. They will want to be around you. They will listen to you. They will become excited when you communicate vision. However, if you do not exhibit some of the additional practices and characteristics listed below, you will not reach your leadership potential, and people may not continue to follow you. One of the greatest potential pitfalls for natural leaders is relying on talent alone.

2. RESPECT FOR OTHERS

Dictators and other autocratic leaders rely on violence and intimidation to get people to do what they want. That's not really leadership. In contrast, good leaders rely on respect. They understand that all leadership is voluntary. When leaders show respect for others—especially for people who have less power or a lower position than theirs—they gain respect from others. And people *want* to follow people they respect greatly.

Gaining respect from others follows a pattern:

When people respect you as a person, they *admire* you.
When they respect you as a friend, they *love* you.
When they respect you as a leader, they *follow* you.

If you continually respect others and consistently lead them well, you will continue to have followers.

3. COURAGE

One thing that caused everyone to respect Harriet Tubman so much was her tremendous courage. She was determined that she was going to succeed, or she was going to die trying. She didn't care about the danger. Her mission was clear, and she was absolutely fearless.

Former U.S. Secretary of State Henry Kissinger remarked, "A leader does not deserve the name unless he is willing occasionally to stand alone." Good leaders do what's right, even at the risk of failure, in the face of great danger, and under the brunt of relentless criticism. I can't think of even one great leader from history who was without courage. Can you? A leader's courage has great value: it gives followers hope.

4. SUCCESS

Success is very attractive. People are naturally drawn to it. It's one reason that people in our society are so focused on celebrities' lives, they cheer for their favorite sports team, and they follow the careers of rock stars.

Success is even more important when it applies to the people who lead us. People respect others' accomplishments. And it's hard to argue with a good track record. When leaders are successful in their own endeavors, people respect them. When they succeed in leading the team to victory, then followers believe they can do it again. As a result, followers follow them because they want to be part of success in the future.

5. LOYALTY

We live in an era of free agency. Professional athletes hop from team to team, looking for the best deal. CEOs negotiate ridiculously high financial packages and then bail out as millionaires when things go wrong. The average worker, according to one source, will change occupations ten times by the time he reaches age thirty-six.[2]

In a culture of constant change, turnover, and transition, loyalty is an asset. When leaders stick with the team until the job is done, remain loyal to the organization when the going gets rough, and look out for followers even when it hurts them, followers respect them and their actions.

6. VALUE ADDED TO OTHERS

Perhaps the greatest source of respect for a leader comes from his or her dedication to adding value to others. Because I've already discussed this extensively in the Law of Addition, I probably don't need to say much here. But you can be sure that followers value leaders who add value to them. And their respect for them carries on long after the relationship has ended.

If you want to measure how much respect you have as a leader, the first thing you should do is to look at who you attract. Dennis A. Peer remarked, "One measure of leadership is the caliber of people who choose to follow you." The second thing you should do is to see how your people respond when you ask for commitment or change.

When leaders are respected and they ask for commitment, their people step up and sign up. They are ready to take risks, charge the hill, put in long hours, or do whatever else is necessary to get the job done. Likewise, when respected leaders ask for change, followers are willing to embrace it. But when leaders who are not respected ask for commitment or change, people doubt, they question, they make excuses, or they simply walk away. It is very hard for a leader who hasn't earned respect to get other people to follow.

DISCUSS

Answer the following questions and discuss your answers when you meet with your team.

1. *Under what circumstances would a strong leader follow a weaker leader?*

_____

_____

_____

2. *Briefly describe the three phases that most groups go through when they first come together.*

_____

_____

_____

3. *Do you agree that in most cases people choose to follow leaders who they respect? Explain.*

_____

_____

_____

4. *How do you determine the strongest leader in the group?*

_____

_____

_____

5. *From your own experience or observation, describe what happens when two strong leaders are placed in the same group.*

_____

_____

_____

6. *Think about a current group in which you are voluntarily participating. Why is the person who is leading the group the leader? What form of respect do you have for the leader (position, friend, admiration, leadership, past accomplishments)?*

_____

_____

_____

7. *How do you react when you are placed in a group of strong leaders?*

_____

_____

_____

8. *What are you doing or what will you start to do to increase your level or respect among the people you interact with often or daily?*

_____

_____

_____

APPLY

1. Think about the last time you asked employees, followers, or volunteers for commitment to something you were leading or to changing something they were doing. What was their response? In general, how readily do people rally to you in either of those situations? That can be used as a fairly accurate gauge of your leadership level.

2. Take a look at the qualities that help a leader to gain respect:

*   Leadership ability (natural ability)
*   Respect for others
*   Courage
*   Success record

- Faithfulness
- Value added to others

Rank yourself in each area on a scale of 1 (low) to 10 (high). One of the best ways to raise your "leadership number" is to improve in each area. In one sentence for each, write a practice, habit, or goal that will help you to improve in that area. Then work for a month on each to make it a regular part of your life.

3. One of my favorite definitions of success is having the respect of those closest to me. I believe that if my family (who knows me the best) and my closest coworkers (who work with me every day) have respect for me, then I am a success and my leadership will be effective.

If you have the courage, ask the people in your life who are closest to you what they respect most about you. And ask them to tell you in which areas you most need to grow. Then determine to improve based on their honest feedback.

TAKE ACTION

Having the respect of those closest to you is priceless. I think success is having the people who know me the best, respect me the most. Respect is not always the result of having other people agree with you, and because we are all unique individuals we are not going to agree on everything. But gaining the respect of the people who know us the best—our success and failures, beliefs and convictions, strengths and weakness, character and motives—is an accomplishment.

This week gather together three of your friends for a discussion. Come up with at least five situations that you and your friends might find yourself in as a group. (Example: planning a trip, entering a business venture, experiencing a medical emergency, teaming up to play a sport, etc.) For each situation, have each person tell which person in the group they would most likely follow and why. List the situations you and your friends come up with below, and list the names of who was mentioned as the leader for each situation.

Situation: Leader:

_____   _____

_____   _____

_____   _____

_____   _____

_____   _____

_____   _____

From this exercise, recognize that different people take the leadership position at different times depending on their skills, personality, and leadership qualities.

Who was named the leader the most times? Why?

_____

_____

_____

Who was named the leader the fewest times? Why?

_____

_____

_____

How often were you named as the person they would follow? What does that say about your leadership? How could you gain more of their respect?

_____

_____

_____

8

THE LAW OF INTUITION

Leaders Evaluate Everything with a Leadership Bias

DURING THE DECADE THAT I'VE SPOKEN TO AUDIENCES ABOUT THE 21 Laws of Leadership, I've found that the Law of Intuition is the most difficult to teach. When I talk about it, natural leaders get it instantly, learned leaders get it eventually, and non-leaders just look at me blankly.

Leaders look at things differently than others do. They evaluate everything according to their leadership bias. They possess leadership intuition that informs everything they do. It is an inseparable part of who they are.

READ

Whenever leaders face a problem, they automatically measure it—and begin solving it—using the Law of Intuition. They evaluate everything with a leadership bias. For example, leadership intuition came into play in recent years at Apple Computer. Just about everybody knows the success story of Apple. The company was created in 1976 by Steve Jobs and Steve Wozniak in a garage. Just four years later, the business went public, opening at twenty-two dollars a share and selling 4.6 million shares. It made more than forty employees and investors millionaires overnight.

But Apple's story hasn't been all positive. Since those early years, Apple's success, stock value, and ability to capture customers have fluctuated wildly. Jobs left Apple in 1985, having been pushed out in a battle with CEO John Sculley, the former Pepsi president whom Jobs had recruited in 1983. Sculley was followed by Michael Spindler in 1993 and then Gilbert Amelio in 1996. None of them was able to reestablish Apple's previous success. In its glory days, Apple had sold 14.6 percent of all personal computers in the United States. By 1997, sales were down to 3.5 percent. That was when Apple again looked to the leadership of its original founder, Steve Jobs, for help. The failing company believed he could save it.

Jobs intuitively reviewed the situation and immediately took action. He knew that improvement was impossible without a change in leadership, so he quickly dismissed all but two of the previous board members and installed new ones. He made changes in the executive leadership. And he fired the company's ad agency and held a competition for the account among three firms.

He also refocused the company. Jobs wanted to get back to the basics of what Apple had always done best: use its individuality to create products that made a difference. At the time Jobs said, "We've reviewed the road map of new products and axed more than 70% of the projects, keeping the 30% that were gems. Plus we're adding new ones that are a whole new paradigm of looking at computers."[1]

None of those actions was especially surprising. But Jobs also did something that really showed the Law of Intuition in action. He read Apple's situation and made a leadership decision that went absolutely against the grain of Apple's previous thinking. It was an incredible intuitive leadership leap. Jobs created a strategic alliance with the man whom Apple employees considered to be their archenemy—Bill Gates. Jobs explained, "I called Bill and said Microsoft and Apple should work more closely together, but we have this issue to resolve, this intellectual-property dispute. Let's resolve it."

They negotiated a deal quickly, which settled Apple's lawsuit against Microsoft. Gates promised to pay off Apple and invest $150 million in nonvoting stock. That cleared the way for future partnership and brought much-needed capital to the company. It was something only an intuitive leader would have done. Apple's stock value immediately went up 33 percent. And in time, Apple regained some of the prestige it had lost over the years.

In 2001, Jobs made another leadership move based on his intuition. While other computer manufacturers were pursuing PDAs, he was looking at music. And when an independent contractor and hardware expert named Tony Fadell approached Apple with an idea for an MP3 player and a music sales company, Apple embraced it, even though several other companies had rejected it. Fadell was hired on, and they began working on what would eventually be known as the iPod.

Jobs involvement with the iPod is an indication of his leadership intuition. Ben Knauss, who was on the inside of the project, says, "The interesting thing about the iPod, is that since it started, it had 100 percent of Steve Jobs' time. Not many projects get that. He was heavily involved in every single aspect of the project."[2] Why did Jobs do that? Because his intuition as a leader made him understand the impact that the device could make. It was consistent with his vision for creating a digital lifestyle.

Jobs has been right on. Sales have been phenomenal and have exceeded the company's computer sales. Apple was making a profit while other technology companies suffered. By spring of 2002, Apple had shipped more than 10 million units.[3] By the end of 2005, Apple possessed 75 percent of the world market for digital music players![4]

OBSERVE

Steve Jobs story is a reminder that leadership is really more art than science. The principles of leadership are constant, but the application changes with every leader and every situation. That's why it requires intuition. Without it, leaders get blindsided, and that's one of the worst things that can happen to a leader.

1. *Why did Steve Jobs create an alliance with Bill Gates?*

_____

_____

_____

2. *Define intuition.*

_____

_____

_____

3. *How does the amount of time a leader has to make a decision relate to the Law of Intuition?*

_____

_____

_____

4. *In your profession or area of service, how has leadership intuition accelerated the success of one organization over another?*

_____

_____

_____

LEARN

Because of their intuition, leaders evaluate everything with a leadership bias. People born with natural leadership ability are especially strong in the area of leadership intuition. Others have to work hard to develop and hone it. But either way, intuition comes from two things: the combination of natural ability, which comes in a person's areas of strength, and learned skills. It is an informed intuition, and it causes leadership issues to jump out to a leader in a way that they don't with others.

I regard leadership intuition as the ability of a leader to read what's going on. For that reason, I say that leaders are readers:

LEADERS ARE READERS OF THEIR SITUATION

Today I wear many hats. I write, speak, mentor, and network. I also own two companies. Although I speak with the presidents of my companies on a weekly basis, they run the day-to-day operations, and I go to the office only occasionally.

Recently John Hull, the president and CEO of EQUIP, commented, "John, when you come in to the office, you reenter our world very easily." I thought that was an interesting choice of words, so I asked what he meant.

"You are very aware of the atmosphere and environment," he explained. "You ask good questions and quickly fall in step with us on our journey. It's never awkward when you return to the office." As I reflected, I realized what he was describing was my use of leadership intuition.

In all kinds of circumstances, leaders pick up on details that might elude others. They "tune in" to leadership dynamics. Many leaders describe this as an ability to "smell" things in their organization. They can sense people's attitudes. They are able to detect the chemistry of a team. They can tell when things are humming and when they're winding down or getting ready to grind to a halt. They don't need to sift through stats, read reports, or examine a balance sheet. They know the situation *before* they have all the facts. That is the result of their leadership intuition.

LEADERS ARE READERS OF TRENDS

Most followers are focused on their current work. They think in terms of tasks at hand, projects, or specific goals. That is as it should be. Most managers are concerned with efficiency and effectiveness. They often possess a broader view than employees, thinking in terms of weeks, months, or even years. But leaders take an even broader view. They look years, even decades ahead.

Everything that happens around us does so in the context of a bigger picture. Leaders have the ability—and responsibility—to step back from what's happening at the moment and to discern not only where the organization has been, but also where it is headed. Sometimes they can accomplish this through analysis, but often the best leaders sense it first and find data to explain it later. Their intuition tells them that something is happening, that conditions are changing, and that trouble or opportunity is coming. Leaders must always be a few steps ahead of their best people, or they're not really leading. They can do that only if they are able to read trends.

LEADERS ARE READERS OF THEIR RESOURCES

A major difference between leaders and everyone else is the way they see resources. A good worker encounters a challenge and thinks, *What can I do to help?* A high achiever asks, *How can I solve this problem?* A peak performer wonders, *What must I do to reach the next level so that I can overcome this?*

Leaders think differently. They think in terms of resources and how to maximize them. They see a challenge, problem, or opportunity, and they think, *Who is the best person to take this on? What resources—raw materials, technology, information, and so forth—do we possess that will help us? What will this take financially? How can I encourage my team to achieve success?*

Leaders see everything with a leadership bias. Their focus is on mobilizing people and leveraging resources to achieve their goals rather than on using their own individual efforts. Leaders who want to succeed maximize every asset and resource they have for the benefit of their organization. For that reason, they are continually aware of what they have at their disposal.

LEADERS ARE READERS OF PEOPLE

President Lyndon Johnson once said that when you walk into a room, you don't belong in politics if you can't tell who's for you and who's against you. That statement also applies to any other kind of leader. Intuitive leaders can sense what's happening among people and know their hopes, fears, and concerns. They can sense what's happening in a room—whether there's curiosity, doubt, reluctance, anticipation, or relief.

Reading people is perhaps the most important intuitive skill leaders can possess. After all, if what you are doing doesn't involve people, it's not leadership. And if you aren't persuading people to follow, you aren't really leading.

LEADERS ARE READERS OF THEMSELVES

Finally, good leaders develop the ability to read themselves. Poet James Russell Lowell observed, "No one can produce great things who is not thoroughly sincere in dealing with himself." Leaders must know not only their own strengths and blind spots, skills and weaknesses, but also their current state of mind. Why? Because leaders can hinder progress just as easily as they can help create it. In fact, it's easier to damage an organization than it is to build one. We've all seen excellent organizations that took generations to build begin falling apart in a matter of years.

When leaders become self-centered, pessimistic, or rigid in their thinking, they often hurt their organizations because they are likely to fall into the trap of thinking they cannot or should not change. And once that happens, the organization has a hard time becoming better. Its decline is inevitable.

THREE LEVELS OF LEADERSHIP INTUITION

If you're saying to yourself, *I'd like to be able to read these dynamics in my organization, but I just don't see things intuitively,* don't despair. The good news is that you can improve your leadership intuition, even if you are not a natural born leader. As I've already mentioned, leadership intuition is *informed* intuition. The less natural leadership talent you have, the more you will need to make up for it by developing skills and gaining experience. They can help you to develop thinking patterns, and thinking patterns can be learned.

I've found that all people fit into three major intuition levels:

1. THOSE WHO NATURALLY UNDERSTAND LEADERSHIP

Some people are born with exceptional leadership gifts. They instinctively understand people and know how to move them from point A to point B. Even when they're kids, they act as leaders. Watch them on the playground, and you can see other kids following them. People with natural leadership intuition can build upon it and become world-class leaders of the highest caliber.

2. THOSE WHO CAN BE NURTURED TO UNDERSTAND LEADERSHIP

Most people fall into this category. They have adequate people skills, and if they are teachable, they can develop intuition. Leadership can be learned. However, people who don't try to improve their leadership and never work to develop their intuition are condemned to being blindsided in their leadership for the rest of their lives.

3. THOSE WHO WILL NEVER UNDERSTAND LEADERSHIP

I believe nearly everyone is capable of developing leadership skills and intuition. But occasionally, I run across someone who doesn't seem to have a leadership bone in his body *and* who has no interest in developing the skills necessary to lead. This isn't you because these people never pick up a leadership book.

DISCUSS

Answer the following questions and discuss your answers when you meet with your team.

1. *What creates intuition?*

    _____
    _____
    _____

2. *Do you agree with the author that intuition is not only natural but can also be developed? Explain.*

    _____
    _____
    _____

3. *Describe a situation in which leadership intuition affected your organization.*

    _____
    _____
    _____

4. *At which level of leadership are you? How has your intuition affected your performance and leadership ability?*

    _____
    _____
    _____

5. *Which presents the biggest challenge for you: accurately reading your situation, tends, your resources, other people, or yourself? How can you improve your intuition in this area?*

    _____
    _____
    _____

APPLY

1. How are you when it comes to trusting your intuition? Are you a facts or feeling person? To become better at the Law of Intuition, you must first be willing to *trust* your intuition. Begin by working within your areas of greatest strength.

First, determine which is your strongest natural talent. Second, participate in that talent, paying attention to your feelings, instincts, and intuition. When do you know something is "right" before you have evidence? How can you tell when you're "on"? Do your instincts in this area ever betray you? If so, when and why? Get to know your aptitude for intuition where you are strong before trying to develop it in leadership.

2. One of the most important abilities in leadership is reading people. How would you rate yourself in this area? Can you tell what others are feeling? Can you sense when people are upset? Happy? Confused? Angry? Do you anticipate what others are thinking?

If this is not an area of strength for you, then work on improving by doing these things:

- Read books on relationships.
- Engage more people in conversations.
- Become a people watcher.

3. Train yourself to think in terms of mobilizing people and harnessing resources. Think about current projects or goals. Now imagine how you can accomplish them *without* doing any of the work yourself except for recruiting, empowering, and motivating others.

You may even want to write the following on a note card and keep it in your pocket or organizer:

Who is the best person to take this on?
What resources do we possess that will help us?
What will this take financially?
How can I encourage my team to achieve success?

How you see your world around you is determined by who you are. And while most people will just be accepting of situations, the intuitive leader looks at every situation and asks questions: Why is it this way? Why is it the popular choice? Why does it or why doesn't it work? What other ways could the situation be approached or the problem be solved? The intuitive leader observes and assesses.

Explore a leadership situation that either you or someone else is in where the decisions being made just don't seem right to you. It could be a situation in which you are the leader and everyone around you is telling you things are fine, but you still have some hesitations. Or it could be a situation in which you think another leader handled a situation incorrectly. Look at different ways the situation could be approached by answering the following questions:

1. What is the situation?
2. What is the popular choice? Why?
3. Why does it or doesn't it work?
4. What is your leadership intuition telling you?
5. What leadership law might it be violating?
6. Is the job being done as well as it could be?
7. Is what's being done damaging relationships?
8. What other way could the situation be approached or the problem be solved?

9

THE LAW OF MAGNETISM

Who You Are Is Who You Attract

Y ou've probably heard the saying, "Birds of a feather flock together." And maybe you've already found this to be true. When you were in school, you might have recognized that good students spent time with good students, people who only wanted to play stuck together, and so on. Well, this idea is also true when it comes to leadership. Who is on your team is seldom determined by what you want, but more by who you are. In order to build a strong team, you must understand the *Law of Magnetism.*

READ

One of the most vivid examples of the Law of Magnetism is found in American history among the military leaders of the Civil War. When the Southern states seceded, there were questions about which side many of the generals would fight for. Robert E. Lee was considered the best general in the nation, and President Lincoln actually offered him command of the Union army. But Lee would never consider fighting against his native Virginia. He declined the offer and joined the Confederacy—and the best generals in the land followed him.

If Lee had chosen to lead an army for the Union instead, many other good generals would have followed him north. As a result, the war probably would have been much shorter. Some speculate that it might have lasted two years instead of five—and hundreds of thousands of lives would have been saved. It just goes to show you that the better leader you are, the better leaders you will attract. And that has an incredible impact on everything you do.

OBSERVE

Al McGuire, former head basketball coach of Marquette University, once said, "A team should be an extension of the coach's personality. My teams were arrogant and obnoxious." It's more than a matter of "should be"—teams cannot help being an extension of their leader's personality.

1. *How did Lee's choice to join the Confederacy affect the Civil War?*

    _____

    _____

    _____

2. *Why are a leader's choices so important?*

    _____

    _____

    _____

3. *Do you agree with the author's statement that the team is an extension of the leader's personality? Give an example that supports your answer.*

    _____

    _____

    _____

4. *Give an example of how leaders attract people like themselves from your own industry or area of service.*

_____

_____

_____

LEARN

Maybe you've started thinking about the people that you have attracted in your organization. You might say to yourself, *Wait a minute. I can name twenty things that make my people different from me.* And my response would be, "Of course, you can." We're all individuals. But the people who are drawn to you probably have more similarities than differences, especially in a few key areas.

Take a look at the following characteristics. If you have recruited and hired a staff, you will probably find that you and the people who follow you share common ground in several of these key areas:

GENERATION

Most organizations reflect the characteristics of their key leaders, and that includes their age. During the dot-com boom of the 1990s, thousands of companies were founded by people in their twenties and early thirties. And who did they hire? Others in their twenties and thirties. In just about any type of organization, most of the time the people who come on board are similar in age to the leaders who hire them. Often that occurs within departments. Sometimes it occurs company-wide.

ATTITUDE

Rarely have I seen positive and negative people attracted to one another. People who view life as a series of opportunities and exciting challenges don't want to hear others talk about how bad things are all the time. I know that's true for me. And not only do people attract others with similar attitudes, but their attitudes tend to become alike. Attitude is one of the most contagious qualities a human being possesses. People with good attitudes tend to make people around them feel more positive. Those with a terrible attitude tend to bring others down.

BACKGROUND

In the chapter on the Law of Process, I wrote about Theodore Roosevelt. One of his memorable accomplishments is his daring charge up San Juan Hill with the Rough Riders during the Spanish-American War. Roosevelt personally recruited that all-volunteer cavalry company, and it was said to be a remarkably peculiar group of people. It was comprised primarily of two types of men: wealthy aristocrats from the Northeast and cowboys from the Wild West. Why? Because TR was an aristocratic-born, Harvard-educated New Yorker who turned himself into a real-life cowboy and big-game hunter in the Dakotas of the West. He was a strong and genuine leader in both worlds, and as a result, he attracted both kinds of people.

People attract—and are attracted to—others of similar background. Blue-collar workers tend to stick together. Employers tend to hire people of the same race. People with education tend to respect and value others who are also well educated. This natural magnetism is so strong that organizations that value diversity have to fight against it.

In the NFL, for example, the team owners are white, and for decades, all the head coaches were white. But because members of the league valued racial diversity, they put into place a diversity policy requiring teams to include at least one minority candidate in the interview process when hiring head coaches. That policy has helped more highly qualified African-American head coaches to be hired. (But other than in the area of race, the *background* of all the coaches remains strikingly similar.)

VALUES

People are attracted to leaders whose values are similar to their own. Think about the people who flocked to President John F. Kennedy after he was elected in 1960. He was a young idealist who wanted to change the world, and he attracted people with a similar profile. When he formed the Peace Corps and called people to service, saying, "Ask not what your country can do for you; ask what you can do for your country," thousands of young, idealistic people stepped forward to answer the challenge.

It doesn't matter whether the shared values are positive or negative. Either way, the attraction is equally strong. Think about someone like Adolf Hitler. He was a very strong leader (as you can judge by his level of influence). But his values were rotten to the core. What kinds of people did he attract? Leaders with similar values: Hermann Goering, founder of the Gestapo; Joseph Goebbels, a bitter anti-Semite who ran Hitler's propaganda machine; Reinhard Heydrich, second in command of the Nazi secret police, who ordered mass executions of Nazi opponents; and Heinrich Himmler, chief of the SS and director of the Gestapo who initiated the systematic execution of Jews. They were all strong leaders, and they were all utterly evil men. The Law of Magnetism is powerful. Whatever character you possess is what you will likely find in the people who follow you.

ENERGY

It's a good thing that people with similar levels of energy are attracted to one another because when you pair a high-energy person with a low-energy person and ask them to work closely together, they can drive one another crazy. The high-energy person thinks the low-energy one is lazy, and the low-energy person thinks the high-energy one is insane.

GIFTEDNESS

People do not go out looking for mediocre leaders to follow. People are attracted to talent and excellence, especially in their area of giftedness. They are most likely to respect and follow someone who possesses their kind of talent. Businesspeople want to follow bosses with skill in building an organization and making a profit. Football players want to follow coaches with great football talent. Creative people want to follow leaders who are willing to think outside the box. Like attracts like. That may seem pretty obvious. Yet I've met many leaders who expect highly talented people to follow them, even though they neither possess nor express value for those people's giftedness.

LEADERSHIP ABILITY

Finally, the people you attract will have leadership ability similar to your own. As I said in discussing the Law of Respect, people naturally follow leaders stronger than themselves. But you also have to factor in the Law of Magnetism, which states that who you are is who you attract. If you are a 7 when it comes to leadership, you are more likely to draw 5s and 6s to you than 2s and 3s. The leaders you attract will be similar in style and ability to you.

DISCUSS

Answer the following questions and discuss your answers when you meet with your team.

1. *Why wasn't Abraham Lincoln able to attract Robert E. Lee to the Union Army? Which common ground reason did Lee's reason fall into?*

_____

_____

_____

2. *Give an example of how background can attract people to certain companies.*

_____

_____

_____

3. *How have the six common-ground areas played a part in the makeup and growth of your organization?*

_____

_____

_____

4. *Which of the common-ground areas has the strongest draw in deciding whom you follow? Explain.*

_____

_____

_____

5. *Which of the common-ground areas do you find attracts the most people to you? Give an example.*

_____

_____

_____

6. *How has your ability to attract others positively or negatively affected your leadership?*

_____

_____

_____

7. *How can you work to become a more magnetic leader?*

_____

_____

_____

APPLY

1. Based on who you are attracting, you may need to grow in the areas of character and leadership. Find mentors willing and able to help you grow in each area. Good candidates as a character mentor could be a pastor or spiritual advisor, a professional whose ability you respect, or a professional coach. Ideally, your leadership mentor should work in the same or a similar profession and be several steps ahead of you in his or her career.

2. If you are already attracting the kinds of people you desire, then it's time to take your leadership to the next level. Work at staffing your weaknesses and recruiting people who will complement your leadership in the area of skills. Write a list of your five greatest strengths when it comes to skills. Then write your five greatest weaknesses.

Now it's time to create a profile of who you are looking for. Start with giftedness that corresponds to your weaknesses. Add to that values and attitude that are similar to yours. Also consider whether age, background, and education are factors. Will it help if they are different? Finally, look for someone who is potentially a good leader or at the very least understands and appreciates how leadership works. Few things are more frustrating to a good leader than a partner with a bureaucratic mind-set.

TAKE ACTION

Effective leaders are always on the lookout for good people. I think each of us carries around a mental list of what kind of people we would like to have in our organization or department. Think about it. Do you know who you're looking for right now? What is your profile of perfect employees? What qualities would they possess? Would you want them to be aggressive and entrepreneurial? Are you looking for leaders? Do you care whether they are in their twenties, forties, or sixties? Stop right now, take a moment, and make a list of the qualities you'd like in the people on your team. Do it now before you read any farther.

My People Would Have These Qualities

_____

_____

_____

_____

_____

_____

_____

Now, what will determine whether the people you want are the people you get, whether they will possess the qualities you desire? You may be surprised by the answer. Believe it or not, who you attract is not determined by what you *want*. It's determined by who you *are*.

Go back to the list you just made, and for each characteristic you identified, decide whether you possess that quality. For example, if you wrote that you would like "great leaders" and you are an excellent leader, that's a match. Put a check (÷) by it. But if your leadership is no better than average, put an X and write "only average leader" next to it. If you wrote that you want people who are "entrepreneurial" and you possess that quality, put a check. Otherwise, mark it with an X, and so on. Now review the whole list.

If you see a whole bunch of Xs, then you're in trouble because the people you describe are not the type who will want to follow you. In most situations unless you take strong measures to counteract it, you draw people to you who possess the same qualities you do. That's the Law of Magnetism: who you are is who you attract.

What can you do to possess the qualities on your list that you put an X next to? Who can you learn from? What resources would help you? Create a plan to improve yourself.

10

THE LAW OF CONNECTION

Leaders Touch a Heart Before They Ask for a Hand

FOR LEADERS TO BE EFFECTIVE, THEY NEED TO CONNECT WITH PEOPLE. Why? Because you first have to touch people's hearts before you ask them for a hand. That is the Law of Connection. All great leaders and communicators recognize this truth and act on it almost instinctively. You can't move people to action unless you first move them with emotion.

READ

In 1972 I was faced with a very difficult situation. I was moving to Lancaster, Ohio, to accept the leadership of a church there. It was going to be a big step up in responsibility for me. Before I accepted the position, I learned that the church had just gone through a big battle related to a building project. Heading up one of the factions was the number one influencer in the church, a man named Jim. I also heard that Jim had a reputation for being negative and something of a maverick. He liked to use his influence to move the people in directions that didn't always help the organization.

Because the previous leader of the church had faced opposition from Jim more than a few times, I knew that I needed to win him over. Otherwise, I would always have conflict with him. If you want someone on your side, don't try to convince him— connect with him. That's what I was determined to do. So the first thing I did when I got to my new position was to make an appointment to meet Jim in my office.

I admit I was not looking forward to meeting Jim. He was a big man—six feet four inches tall and about 250 pounds. He was very intimidating. Further, he was sixty-five years old, and I was only twenty-five. The meeting had the potential to go ugly.

"Jim," I said as he sat in my office, "I know you're the influencer in this church, and I want you to know that I've decided I'm going to do everything in my power to build a good relationship with you. I'd like to meet with you every Tuesday for lunch at the Holiday Inn to talk through issues. While I'm the leader here, I'll never take any decision to the people without first discussing it with you. I really want to work with you.

"But I also want you to know that I've heard you're a very negative person," I continued, "and that you like to fight battles. If you decide to work against me, I'll guess we'll just have to be on opposite sides. And because you have so much influence, I know you'll win most of the time, at least in the beginning. But I'm going to develop relationships with people and draw new people to this church. This church will grow, and someday I'll have greater influence than you.

"But I don't want to battle you," I confided. "You're sixty-five years old right now. Let's say you've got another ten to fifteen years of good health and productivity ahead of you. If you want, you can make these years your very best and make your life count.

"We can do a lot of great things together at this church," I summed up, "but the decision is yours."

When I finished, Jim didn't say a word. He got up from his seat, walked into the hall, and stopped to take a drink at the water fountain. I followed him out and waited. I didn't know whether he was going to dress me down, declare war, or tell me to take a hike.

After a long time, Jim stood up straight and turned around. When he did, I could see that tears were rolling down his cheeks. And then he gave me a great big bear hug and said, "You can count on me to be on your side."

And Jim did get on my side. As it turned out, he did live about another ten years, and because he was willing to help me, a young kid with a vision, we accomplished many positive things together. But it never would have happened if I hadn't had the courage to try to make a connection with him that first day in my office.

OBSERVE

Good leaders work at connecting with others all of the time, whether they are communicating to an entire organization or working with a single individual. The stronger the relationship you form with followers, the greater the connection you forge—and the more likely those followers will be to want to help you. I used to tell my staff, "People don't care how much you know until they know how much you care." They would groan because they heard me say it so much, but they recognized that it was true nonetheless. You develop credibility with people when you connect with them and show that you genuinely care and want to help them. And as a result, they usually respond in kind and want to help you.

1. *How did John connect with Jim?*

   _____
   _____
   _____

2. *Why is it important to connect with your team?*

   _____
   _____
   _____

3. *Do you agree with the author that leaders must touch a heart before they ask for a hand? Explain or give an example.*

   _____
   _____
   _____

4. *In your profession or area of service, who has mastered the Law of Connection? How do you react when you hear this person speak?*

_____

_____

_____

LEARN

One key to connecting with others is recognizing that even in a group, you have to relate to people as individuals. General Norman Schwarzkopf remarked, "I have seen competent leaders who stood in front of a platoon and all they saw was a platoon. But great leaders stand in front of a platoon and see it as 44 individuals, each of whom has aspirations, each of whom wants to live, each of whom wants to do good."[1]

I've had the opportunity to speak to some wonderful audiences during the course of my career. The largest have been in stadiums with more than sixty thousand people in attendance. Some of my colleagues who also speak for a living have asked me, "How in the world do you speak to that many people?" The secret is simple. I don't try to talk to the thousands. I focus on talking to one person. That's the only way to connect with people. It's the same way when writing a book. I don't think of the millions of people who have read my books. I think of *you*. I believe that if I can connect with you as an individual, then what I have to offer might be able to help you. If I'm not connecting, you'll stop reading and go do something else.

How do you connect? Whether you're speaking in front of a large audience or chatting in the hallway with an individual, the guidelines are the same:

1. CONNECT WITH YOURSELF

You must know who you are and have confidence in yourself if you desire to connect with others. People don't heed the call of an uncertain trumpet. Be confident and be yourself. If you don't believe in who you are and where you want to lead, work on that before doing anything else.

2. COMMUNICATE WITH OPENNESS AND SINCERITY

People can smell a phony a mile away. Legendary NFL coach Bill Walsh observed, "Nothing is more effective than sincere, accurate praise, and nothing is more lame than a cookie-cutter compliment." Authentic leaders connect.

3. KNOW YOUR AUDIENCE

When you work with individuals, knowing your audience means learning people's names, finding out about their histories, asking about their dreams. When you communicate to an audience, you learn about the organization and its goals. You want to speak to what *they* care about, not just what you care about.

4. LIVE YOUR MESSAGE

Perhaps the most important thing you can do as a leader and communicator is to practice what you preach. That's where credibility comes from. Plenty of people out in the marketplace are willing to say one thing to an audience but do something else. They don't last.

5. GO TO WHERE THEY ARE

As a communicator, I dislike any kind of barrier to communication. I don't like to be too far from my audience or too high above them on a stage. And I definitely don't want any physical barriers between me and the people. But a person's *method* of communication can also be a barrier. Whether I'm speaking from a stage or sitting across from someone in my office, I try to speak the other person's language, to go to that person. I try to be attuned to others' culture, background, education, and so on. I adapt to others; I don't expect them to adapt to me.

6. FOCUS ON THEM, NOT YOURSELF

If you got on an elevator with me and asked me to tell you the secret to good communication before I got off at the next floor, I'd tell you to focus on others, not yourself. That is the number one problem of inexperienced speakers, and it is also the number one problem of ineffective leaders. You will always connect faster when your focus is not on yourself.

7. BELIEVE IN THEM

It's one thing to communicate to people because you believe you have something of value to say. It's another to communicate with people because you believe they have value. People's opinion of us has less to do with what they see in us than it does with what we can help them see in themselves.

8. OFFER DIRECTION AND HOPE

People expect leaders to help them get where they want to go. But good leaders do that and more. French general Napoleon Bonaparte said, "Leaders are dealers in hope." That is so true. When you give people hope, you give them a future.

Never underestimate the power of making connections and building relationships with people before asking them to follow you. If you've ever studied the lives of notable military commanders, you have probably noticed that the best ones practiced the Law of Connection. I read that during World War I in France, General Douglas MacArthur told a battalion commander before a daring charge, "Major, when the signal comes to go over the top, I want you to go first, before your men. If you do, they'll follow." Then MacArthur removed the Distinguished Service Cross from his uniform and pinned it on the major. He had, in effect, awarded him for heroism before asking him to exhibit it. And of course, the major led his men, they followed him over the top, and they achieved their objective.

Not all military examples of the Law of Connection are quite so dramatic, but they are still effective. For example, it's said that Napoleon made it a practice to know every one of his officers by name and to remember where they lived and which battles they had fought with him. Robert E. Lee was known to visit the men at their campsites the night before any major battle. Often he met the next day's challenges without having slept. More recently, I read about how Norman Schwarzkopf connected with his troops during the first Persian Gulf War. On Christmas in 1990, he spent the day in the mess halls among the men and women who were so far away from their families. In his autobiography, he says,

> I shook hands with everyone in the line, went behind the serving counter to greet the cooks and helpers, and worked my way through the mess hall, hitting every

table, wishing everyone Merry Christmas. Then I went into the second and third dining facilities and did the same thing. I came back to the first mess tent and repeated the exercise, because by this time there was an entirely new set of faces. Then I sat down with some of the troops and had my dinner. In the course of four hours, I must have shaken four thousand hands.2

Schwarzkopf was a general. He didn't have to do that, but he did. He used one of the most effective methods for connecting with others, something I call walking slowly through the crowd. It may sound corny, but it's really true: People don't care how much you know until they know how much you care. As a leader, find times to make yourself available to people. Learn their names. Tell them how much you appreciate them. Find out how they're doing. And most important, listen. Leaders who relate to their people and really connect with them are leaders that people will follow to the ends of the earth.

When a leader truly has done the work to connect with his people, you can see it in the way the organization functions. Employees exhibit loyalty and a strong work ethic. The vision of the leader becomes the aspiration of the people. The impact is incredible.

One of the companies I admire is Southwest Airlines. The company has been successful and profitable while other airlines have filed for bankruptcy and folded. The person responsible for the initial success of the organization and the creation of its culture is Herb Kelleher, the company's founder and current executive chairman of the board.

I love what Southwest's employees did on Boss's Day in 1994 because it shows the kind of connection Kelleher made with his people. They took out a full-page ad in *USA Today* and addressed the following message to Kelleher:

Thanks, Herb
For remembering every one of our names.
For supporting the Ronald McDonald House.
For helping load baggage on Thanksgiving.
For giving everyone a kiss (and we mean everyone).
For listening.

For running the only profitable major airline.
For singing at our holiday party.
For singing only once a year.
For letting us wear shorts and sneakers to work.
For golfing at The LUV Classic with only one club.
For outtalking Sam Donaldson.
For riding your Harley Davidson into Southwest Headquarters.
For being a friend, not just a boss.
Happy Boss's Day from Each One of Your 16,000 Employees[3]

A display of affection like that occurs only when a leader has worked hard to connect with his people.

Don't ever underestimate the importance of building relational bridges between yourself and the people you lead. There's an old saying: to lead yourself, use your head; to lead others, use your heart. That's the nature of the Law of Connection. Always touch a person's heart before you ask him for a hand.

DISCUSS

Answer the following questions and discuss your answers when you meet with your team.

1. How does the ability to connect with others relate to leadership?

_____

_____

_____

2. How long does it normally take to connect with someone? Describe the signs of connection.

_____

_____

_____

3. Which of the Eight Keys to Connection do you do best? Which is an area of weakness? Why?

_____

_____

_____

4. Are there other aspects to connection? Why do you agree or disagree with the author's list?

_____

_____

_____

5. How have you connected with someone on your team? Did you initiate the relationship or did they?

_____

_____

_____

6. Up to now, why did you think it was or wasn't important to connect with people in your work environment?

_____

_____

_____

7. How can you initiate healthy work relationships?

_____

_____

_____

APPLY

1. What does it really mean to "connect with yourself"? It means *knowing* and *liking* who you are. Start by measuring your level of self-awareness. Answer each of the following questions:

How would I describe my personality?
What is my greatest character strength?
What is my greatest character weakness?
What is my single greatest asset?
What is my single greatest deficit?
How well do I relate to others (1 to 10)?
How well do I communicate with others (1 to 10)?
How likable am I (1 to 10)?

Now ask three people who know you well to answer the same questions about you. Compare answers. If their answers are significantly different from yours, then you have a blind spot you need to rectify. Engage a mentor, growth and accountability partner, or counselor to help you become more self-aware and to help you value your strengths and deal positively with your weaknesses.

2. Learn to walk slowly through the crowd. When you are out among your employees or coworkers, make relationship building and connecting a priority. Before getting into work matters, make a connection. With people you don't yet know, that may take some time. With people you know well, still take a moment to connect relationally. It may cost you only a few minutes a day, but it will pay huge dividends in the future. And it will make the workplace a more positive environment.

3. Good leaders are good communicators. On a scale of 1 to 10, how would you rate yourself as a public speaker? If you give yourself anything lower than an 8, you need to work on improving your skills. Read books on communication, take a class, or join Toastmasters. And sharpen your skills by practicing your teaching and communicating. If you don't have opportunities to do that on the job, then try volunteering.

TAKE ACTION

When a leader has done the work to connect with his people, you can see it in the way the organization functions. Among employees there is incredible loyalty and a strong work ethic. The vision of the leader becomes the aspiration of the people, and the impact is incredible.

This week, spend time connecting with someone on your team that you don't already know very well. Find an appropriate situation that will allow you to talk about interests outside of work. You could ask the person to join you or a group for lunch. If that's not an option, look to see if the person has anything in their workspace that might be a conversation starter (pictures of family, college memorabilia, collectables or souvenirs in plain sight). Make it a goal to learn three things about the person.

11

THE LAW OF THE INNER CIRCLE

A Leader's Potential Is Determined by Those Closest to Him

WHEN WE SEE ANY INCREDIBLY GIFTED PERSON, IT'S ALWAYS TEMPTING to believe that talent alone made him successful. To think that is to buy in to a lie. Nobody does anything great alone. Leaders do not succeed alone. A leader's potential is determined by those closest to him. What makes the difference is the leader's inner circle.

READ

Lance Armstrong is one of the most talented athletes on the planet. Because of his physical gifts, he has been called a freak of nature. His sport, cycling, is perhaps the most grueling. The Tour de France, which he won an astounding seven times in a row, has been compared to running twenty marathons on twenty consecutive days. Racers cover approximately two thousand miles of often mountainous terrain in a three-week period. On peak race days, they consume as many as ten thousand calories to provide the energy they need.

Armstrong has become a legend as the conqueror of the Tour de France. Writer Michael Specter provides perspective on Armstrong's ability:

> Three types of riders succeed in long stage races like the Tour de France: those who
> excel at climbing but are only adequate in time trials, in which a cyclist races alone

against the clock; those who can win time trials but struggle in the mountains; and cyclists who are moderately good at both. Now there appears to be a fourth group: Armstrong. He has become the best climber in the world . . . And there is no cyclist better at time trials.[1]

Clearly, Armstrong is in a class that few others can approach. His determination is unquestionable. His training regimen is unmatched. His talent is extraordinary. Yet without a team, he would not have won a single Tour title.

Cycling is truly a team sport, though it may not seem that way to the casual observer. During his Tour de France run, Armstrong had an incredible team. Anchoring the team were Chris Carmichael, his coach; and Johan Bruyneel, an ex-cyclist who functioned as the team's sports director and master tactician. Both men were indispensable, since Armstrong tended at first to follow his own less efficient training regimen and execute his own tactics, causing him to lose badly. But once those two inner circle members were in place, Armstrong began to maximize his gift.

Taking the team approach even further, Armstrong's sponsors and equipment suppliers—Trek, Nike, AMD, Bontrager, Shimano, and Oakley—were asked to work together as a group rather than merely contributing as individuals without knowing what the others were doing. It was revolutionary at the time and helped raise the entire team to a higher level. It is now standard practice in professional cycling.

And then, of course, there were the other cyclists who rode with him each year. In 2005, Armstrong's last year, they included José Azevedo of Portugal; Manuel Beltrán, Benjamin Noval, and José Luis Rubiera of Spain; Pavel Padmos of the Czech Republic; Yaroslav Popovych of Ukraine; Paolo Savoldelli of Italy; and George Hincapie of the U.S. "I wanted an experienced team for Lance's last Tour and that was the determining factor," explained Bruyneel.[2] Each person brought unique skills to the team.

"I think we have fielded our strongest team ever with this formation," said Armstrong. "It has many consistent elements from years past, like the Spanish armada for the climbs, strong guys like George, Pavel and Benjamin, the Giro winner in Savoldelli plus a guy like Popo (Popovych) with a very bright future. I look forward to leading this team and attempting to give the great folks at Discovery a yellow jersey."

"Lance is the first to say he would never have won the Tour de France without the help of his teammates," explains the Team Discovery Web site. "Every other rider sacrifices individual glory at the race in order to work for one rider, Lance, which says a lot considering what's at stake. Yet, over the years, Lance delivered every single time following the work of his team, so it goes hand in hand. If the team sacrificed itself and Lance didn't have what it took to come through in the end, we would have had to rethink the plan."[3]

Leaders have to deliver. There is no substitute for performance. But without a good team, they often don't get the opportunity. Their potential is determined by those closest to them. That is the Law of the Inner Circle.

OBSERVE

Leadership expert Warren Bennis said, "The leader finds greatness in the group, and he or she helps the members find it in themselves."[4] Think of any highly effective leader, and you will find someone who surrounded himself with a strong inner circle.

1. *Who is on Armstrong's team?*

_____

_____

_____

2. *Why is it important for Armstrong to recognize his team when he wins?*

_____

_____

_____

3. *Think of someone in your profession or area of service whom you consider successful. How has this person utilized the Law of the Inner Circle?*

_____

_____

_____

4. *How will your potential be affected if you don't form a strong inner circle?*

_____

_____

_____

LEARN

Most people create an inner circle of people. However, they are usually not strategic in doing so. We naturally tend to surround ourselves with either people we like or people with whom we are comfortable. Few people give enough thought to how those closest to them impact their effectiveness or leadership potential. You see it all the time with certain athletes who transition to the professional ranks and entertainers who achieve success professionally. Some self-destruct and never reach their potential, and it can often be attributed to the kind of people they spend their time with.

To practice the Law of the Inner Circle, you must be intentional in your relationship building. You must give thought to the accomplishment of your mission and the success of the people who follow you. Only if you reach your potential as a leader do your people have a chance to reach their potential.

As you consider whether individuals should be in your inner circle, ask yourself the following questions. If you can answer yes to these questions, then they are excellent candidates for your inner circle:

1. Do They Have High Influence with Others?

One key to successful leadership is the ability to influence the people who influence others. How do you do that? By drawing influencers into your inner circle. That was what I did with Jim at the church in Lancaster, Ohio, whom I wrote about in the Law of Connection. Jim was the single most influential person in the organization when I arrived. By building a relationship with Jim and taking him into my inner circle, I was doing two things. First, I was exerting my influence on him—sharing my values, vision, and philosophy of leadership with him. I wanted him to be a carrier of the vision to other people in the organization. Second, I was finding out what he thought. If he had questions or objections to what I wanted to do, I was able to find out about it immediately and work through it with him. And because he had so many years of experience with the people in the organization, he often helped me to navigate around potential landmines I knew nothing about.

2. DO THEY BRING A COMPLEMENTARY GIFT TO THE TABLE?

Because of my leadership gifting, I naturally attract leaders. And I am also highly attracted to leaders. It's said of great baseball hitters that when they get together with other good hitters, all they talk about is hitting. It's similar with good leaders. When they get together, they share their experiences, ask each other questions, and test ideas. But one of the best things I have done in my leadership career is to bring a few key people into my inner circle who possess strengths in my areas of weakness.

One of those people is Linda Eggers, my assistant. I advise young executives that their first and most important hire should be their assistant. In Linda, I have an absolute gem! She has been working with me for twenty years. She has an incredible mind for details, she is tireless, and like "Radar" O'Reilly from *Mash,* she has the ability to anticipate what I need before I realize it. What's more, she now knows me so well that she can speak to others on my behalf, knowing how I would answer questions at least 90 percent of the time.

3. DO THEY HOLD A STRATEGIC POSITION IN THE ORGANIZATION?

Some people belong in your inner circle because of their importance to the organization. If you and they are not working on the same page, the entire organization is in trouble. John Hull certainly fits that description in my life. EQUIP and ISS, organizations he leads for me, cannot function without his leadership. Some of the most significant and effective things I'm doing are being accomplished through EQUIP. The organization has already trained more than a million leaders around the globe and is gearing up to train even more.

If something were to happen at EQUIP that took it in the wrong direction, many things in my life would come to a grinding halt. It could create personal chaos for me.

That's why I have John, who is an outstanding leader, heading up the organization—and why he remains close to me in my inner circle.

4. Do They Add Value to Me and to the Organization?

I discussed in the Law of Addition how people add, subtract, multiply, or divide when it comes to others. The people in your inner circle must be adders or multipliers. They should have a proven track record as assets to the organization. There is a poem by Ella Wheeler Wilcox that my mother used to recite to me when I was growing up:

> There are two kinds of people on earth today,
> Just two kinds of people, no more, I say.
> Not the good and the bad, for 'tis well understood
> That the good are half-bad and the bad are half-good.
> No! The two kinds of people on earth I mean
> Are the people who lift and the people who lean.
> There are two kinds of people on earth today;
> Just two kinds of people, no more, I say.
> Not the sinner and saint, for it's well understood,
> The good are half bad, and the bad are half good. . .
> No; the two kinds of people on earth I mean,
> Are the people who lift, and the people who lean.
> Look only for lifters for your inner circle.

Inner circle members should also add value to you personally. That's not selfish. If they have a negative effect, they will hinder your ability to lead well, and that can hurt your people and the organization.

Someone once told me, "It's lonely at the top, so you had better know why you're there." It's true that leaders carry heavy loads. When you're out front, you can be an easy target. That's why I say, "It's lonely at the top, so you'd better take someone with you." Who could be better than someone who lifts you up, not as a yes-man, but as a solid supporter and friend? Solomon of ancient Israel recognized this truth: "As iron sharpens iron, friends sharpen the minds of each other."[5] Seek for your inner circle people who help you improve.

5. DO THEY POSITIVELY IMPACT OTHER INNER CIRCLE MEMBERS?

I'm a big believer in team chemistry, and if your inner circle is going to work together and function as a team, then you need to take into account how members interact. First, you want them to have a good fit with one another. Just as members of a championship basketball team have complementary skills and compatible roles, you want each inner circle member to have a place in your life where he contributes without stepping on the others' toes.

Second, you want inner circle members to make one another better, to raise one another's game. Sometimes that comes because they encourage one another. Sometimes it happens when they help one another by sharing information and wisdom. And sometimes it comes from friendly competition. No matter how it happens, if they improve the ability of other team members, they also improve your leaders.

IDENTIFY . . . CULTIVATE . . . RECRUIT

There is one more question you need to ask about potential inner circle members. I did not list it as one of the five questions, because a yes in answer to the question does not automatically mean they should be in your inner circle. However, a no would definitely mean they should not. The question is this: Do they display excellence, maturity, and good character in everything they do?

You will be able to answer that question only once you've gotten to know them fairly well, which means you will probably be selecting inner circle members from within your organization. In fact, in most cases you will also need to develop them before they are ready to take their place in that circle. As you look for people and work with them, take the advice of longtime executive and retired president, CEO, and chairman of Agilent Technologies, Ned Barnholt. He believes there are three kinds of people in an organization when it comes to leadership: (1) those who get it almost immediately and they're off and running with it; (2) those who are skeptical and not sure what to do with it; and (3) another third who start out negative and hope it will go away. "I used to spend most of my time with those who were the most negative," says Barnholt, "trying to convince them to change. Now I spend my time with the people in the first [group]. I'm investing in my best assets."[6]

Lee Iacocca says that success comes not from what you know, but from who you know and how you present yourself to each of those people. There is a lot of truth in that. If you want to increase your capacity and maximize your potential as a leader, your first step is always to become the best leader you can. The next is to surround yourself with the best leaders you can find. Never forget that a leader's potential is determined by those closest to him. That's the Law of the Inner Circle. That's the only way you can reach the highest level possible.

DISCUSS

Answer the following questions and discuss your answers when you meet with your team.

1. *Do you agree with the author's list of questions to ask when creating an inner circle? What other qualities would you look for?*

_____

_____

_____

2. *In the past, how have you selected people for your inner circle?*

_____

_____

_____

3. *What are the common characteristics found in the people you surround yourself with?*

_____

_____

_____

4. *Have the people you've chosen to spend time with enhanced your life or made it more difficult? If they've done more harm than good, how must you change your selection process?*

_____

_____

_____

APPLY

1. Do you know who your inner circle members are? Before you have a leadership position, they are the people you seek out for advice, turn to for support, and rely on to help you get things done. When you lead a small staff, all of those employees are also part of your inner circle.

List the names of your inner circle members. Next to each name write what that person contributes. If they do not have a clear role or function, then write what you believe they have *the potential* to contribute. Look for holes and duplications. Then begin looking for people to fill the holes and consider how you might eliminate redundancies. And be prepared to challenge current members with potential to rise to your expectations.

2. Great inner circles do not come together by accident. Effective leaders are continually developing current and future inner circle members. How do they do it?

• They spend extra time with them strategically to mentor them and to develop relationships.
• They give them extra responsibility and place higher expectations on them.

- They give them more credit when things go well and hold them accountable when they don't.

Examine your list of inner circle members to determine whether you are taking these steps with them. If not, make changes. In addition, be sure to use this development strategy with a pool of new potential inner circle members.

3. If you lead a larger staff, then not everyone who works for you will be part of your inner circle. When should you transition to a smaller inner circle, a sort of team within the team?

- When your immediate staff numbers more than seven.
- When you can no longer directly lead everyone.
- In the volunteer world, when others besides paid staff should be in the inner circle.

If this describes your situation, then begin thinking in terms of creating a smaller inner circle group using the same development strategy listed above.

TAKE ACTION

Evaluate your inner circle. List the names of your current inner circle members. Next to each name, explain why that person is a part of your inner circle. What qualities and skills do they bring to the table? What areas are the more equipped in that you? How do their abilities compliment and complete your abilities? How do they support you emotionally? How do they move you closer to your goals for the team?

Inner Circle Member   Contributions

_____   _____

_____   _____

_____   _____

_____   _____

_____   _____

If there are people on your list who add no value or who bring you down, you should consider moving them out of your inner circle.

After identifying your current inner circle members and the qualities and skills they bring to the table, try to identify three more people whom you might want to add to your inner circle. Next to each person's name list the unique skills and qualities they would bring to the group. Look for people who can fill a need that is not already being filled by another member of your inner circle. Remember that your inner circle should be made up of people from different areas of your life so you can receive a well-rounded balance of feedback and insight.

Potential Inner Circle Member   Contributions

_____   _____

_____   _____

_____   _____

_____   _____

_____   _____

12

THE LAW OF EMPOWERMENT

Only Secure Leaders Give Power to Others

THE ONLY WAY TO MAKE YOURSELF *INDISPENSABLE* IS TO MAKE YOURSELF Dispensable. By becoming a secure leader who can give power away, you will make your organization more powerful. But if you disregard the *Law of Empowerment,* your potential will be limited.

READ

Nearly everyone has heard of Henry Ford, the revolutionary automobile industry innovator and legend in American business history. In 1903, he cofounded the Ford Motor Company with the belief that the future of the automobile lay in putting it within the reach of the average American worker. Ford said,

> I will build a motorcar for the multitude. It will be large enough for the family but small enough for the individual to run and care for. It will be constructed of the best materials, by the best men to be hired, after the simplest designs that modern engineering can devise. But it will be so low in price that no man making a good salary will be unable to own one—and enjoy with his family the blessings of hours of pleasure in God's great open spaces.

Henry Ford carried out that vision with the Model T, and it changed the face of twentieth-century American life. By 1914, Ford was producing nearly 50 percent of all automobiles in the United States. The Ford Motor Company looked like an American success story.

However, all of Ford's story is not about positive achievement, and one reason is that he didn't embrace the Law of Empowerment. Henry Ford was so in love with his Model T that he never wanted to change or improve it—nor did he want anyone else to tinker with it. One day when a group of his designers surprised him by presenting him with the prototype of an improved model, Ford furiously ripped its doors off the hinges and proceeded to destroy the car with his bare hands.

For almost twenty years, the Ford Motor Company offered only one design, the Model T, which Henry Ford had personally developed. It wasn't until 1927 that he finally—grudgingly—agreed to offer a new car to the public. The company produced the Model A, but it was incredibly far behind its competitors in technical innovations. Despite its early head start and the incredible lead over its competitors, the Ford Motor Company's market share kept shrinking. By 1931, it was down to only 28 percent, a little more than half of what it produced seventeen years earlier.

Henry Ford was the antithesis of an empowering leader. He continually undermined his leaders and looked over the shoulders of his people. He even created a sociological department within Ford Motor Company to check up on his employees and direct their private lives. As time went by, he became more and more eccentric. He once went into his accounting office and tossed the company's books into the street, saying, "Just put all the money we take in in [sic] a big barrel and when a shipment of material comes in reach into the barrel and take out enough money to pay for it."

Perhaps Ford's most peculiar dealings were with his executives, especially his son Edsel. The younger Ford had worked at the company since he was a boy. As Henry became more eccentric, Edsel worked harder to keep the company going. If it weren't for Edsel, the Ford Motor Company probably would have gone out of business in the 1930s. Henry eventually gave Edsel the presidency of the company, but at the same time he undermined his son. Further, whenever a promising leader was rising up in the company, Henry tore him down. As a result, the company kept losing its best executives. The few who stayed did so because they figured that someday old Henry would die, and Edsel would finally take over and set things right. But that's not what happened. In 1943, Edsel died at age forty-nine.

Edsel's oldest son, the twenty-six-year-old Henry Ford II, quickly left the navy so that he could return to Dearborn, Michigan, and take over the company. At first, he faced opposition from his grandfather's entrenched followers. But within two years, he gathered the support of several key people, received the backing of the board of directors (his mother controlled 41 percent of Ford Motor Company's stock), and convinced his grandfather to step down so that he could become president in his place.

Young Henry was taking over a company that hadn't made a profit in fifteen years. At that time, it was losing $1 million *a day!* The young president knew he was in over his head, so he set out to find leaders. Fortunately, the first group actually approached him. Colonel Charles "Tex" Thornton headed a team of ten men who had worked together at the War Department during World War II. Their contribution to Ford Motor Company was substantial. In the years to come, the group produced six company vice presidents and two presidents.

The second influx of leadership came with the entrance of Ernie Breech, an experienced General Motors executive and the former president of Bendix Aviation. Young Henry hired him to be Ford's executive vice president, a position second to Henry's, with the expectation that he would take command and turn the company around. He succeeded. Breech quickly brought in more than 150 outstanding executives from General Motors, and by 1949, Ford Motor Company was on a roll again. In that year, the company sold more than a million Fords, Mercurys, and Lincolns—the best sales since the Model A.

If Henry Ford II had lived by the Law of Empowerment, the Ford Motor Company might have grown enough to eventually overtake General Motors and become the number one car company again. But only secure leaders are able to give power to others, and Henry felt threatened. The success of Tex Thornton, Ernie Breech, and Lewis Crusoe, a legendary GM executive whom Breech had brought into the company, made Henry worry about his own place at Ford. His position was based not on influence but on his name and his family's control of company stock.

What was Henry's solution? He began pitting one top executive against another, first Thornton against Crusoe. Then after Thornton was fired, he turned Crusoe against Breech. Ford biographers Peter Collier and David Horowitz described the second Henry Ford's method this way:

> Henry's instinct for survival manifested itself as craftiness combined with a kind of weakness. He had endowed Crusoe with the power to do virtually whatever he wished. By withdrawing his grace from Breech and bestowing it on his lieutenant, he had made antagonists of the two men most vital to Ford's success. While Henry had lost confidence in Breech, however, he had left him officially in charge because this increased his own maneuverability. And, as Crusoe's official superior, Breech could be useful if Henry wanted to keep Crusoe in check.[1]

This became a pattern in the leadership of Henry Ford II. Anytime an executive gained power and influence, Henry undercut the person's authority by moving him to a position with less clout, supporting the executive's subordinates, or publicly humiliating him. This maneuver continued all the days Henry II was at Ford. As one Ford president, Lee Iacocca, commented after leaving the company, "Henry Ford, as I would learn firsthand, had a nasty habit of getting rid of strong leaders."

Iacocca says that Henry Ford II once described his leadership philosophy to him, years before Iacocca himself became its target. Ford said, "If a guy works for you, don't let him get too comfortable. Don't let him get cozy or set in his ways. Always do the opposite of what he expects. Keep your people anxious and off-balance."[2]

Both Henry Fords failed to abide by the Law of Empowerment. Rather than identifying leaders, building them up, giving them resources, authority, and responsibility, and then turning them loose to achieve, they alternately encouraged and undermined their best people. Their insecurity made it impossible for them to give power to others. Ultimately, it undermined their personal leadership potential, created havoc in the lives of the people around them, and damaged their organization.

OBSERVE

If leaders want to be successful, they have to be willing to empower others. I like the way President Theodore Roosevelt stated it: "The best executive is the one who has sense enough to pick good men to do what he wants done, and the self-restraint enough to keep from meddling with them while they do it."

1. *Why did the Ford Company lose its market share?*

    _____

    _____

    _____

2. *How did both Henry Ford and Henry Ford II violate the Law of Empowerment? How did this affect their company?*

    _____

    _____

    _____

3. *Give an example of how a leader in your profession or area of service has violated the Law of Empowerment, and how it has affected his or her organization.*

    _____

    _____

    _____

4. *Give an example of how a leader in your profession or area of service has exemplified the Law of Empowerment, and how it has affected his or her organization.*

    _____

    _____

    _____

LEARN

To lead others well, we must help them to reach their potential. That means being on their side, encouraging them, giving them power, and helping them to succeed. That's not traditionally what we're taught about leadership. What were the two leadership games we were taught as kids? King of the Hill and Follow the Leader. What was the object of King of the Hill? To knock other people down so that you can be the leader. And what's the point in Follow the Leader? You do things you *know* followers can't do to separate yourself from them and make yourself look more powerful. The problem with those games is that to win, you have to make all of the other people lose. The games are based on insecurity and are the opposite of the way to raise up leaders.

When I travel to developing countries, I am made especially aware of how alien the idea of empowerment can be to emerging leaders. In cultures where you have to fight to make something of yourself, the assumption often is that you need to fight others to maintain your leadership. But that reflects a scarcity mind-set. The truth is that if you give some of your power away to others, there is still plenty to go around.

When I teach the Law of Empowerment in emerging countries, I usually ask a volunteer to come up so that I can show visually what happens when a leader tries to keep others down instead of raising them up. I ask the volunteer to stand in front of me, and I put my hands on his shoulders. Then I begin pushing him down. The lower I want to push him, the more I have to bend down to do it. As I push him lower, I go lower. That's the same way it is in leadership: to keep others down, you have to go down with them. And when you do that, you lose any power to lift others up.

BARRIERS TO EMPOWERMENT

Leading well is not about enriching yourself—it's about empowering others. Leadership analysts Lynne McFarland, Larry Senn, and John Childress affirm the "empowerment leadership model shifts away from 'position power' to 'people power,' within which all people are given leadership roles so they can contribute to their fullest capacity."[3] Only empowered people can reach their potential. When a leader can't or won't empower others, he creates barriers within the organization that followers cannot overcome. If the barriers remain long enough, then the people give up and stop trying, or they go away to another organization where they can maximize their potential.

When leaders fail to empower others, it is usually due to three main reasons:

THE #1 BARRIER TO EMPOWERMENT: DESIRE FOR JOB SECURITY

The number one enemy of empowerment is the fear of losing what we have. Weak leaders worry that if they help subordinates, they themselves will become dispensable. But the truth is if you are able to continually empower others and help them develop so that they become capable of taking over your job, you will become so valuable to the organization that you become indispensable. That's a paradox of the Law of Empowerment.

What if I work myself out of a job by empowering others, you may ask, *and my superiors don't recognize my contribution?* That can happen in the short term. But if you keep raising up leaders and empowering them, you will develop a pattern of achievement, excellence, and leadership that will be recognized and rewarded. If the teams you lead always seem to succeed, people will figure out that you are leading them well.

THE #2 BARRIER TO EMPOWERMENT: RESISTANCE TO CHANGE

Nobel Prize–winning author John Steinbeck asserted, "It is the nature of man as he grows older to protest against change, particularly change for the better." By its very nature, empowerment brings constant change because it encourages people to grow and innovate. Change is the price of progress. That's not always easy to live with.

Most people don't like change. That's a fact. Yet one of the most important responsibilities of leaders is to continually improve their organizations. As a leader, you must train yourself to embrace change, to desire it, to make a way for it. Effective leaders are not only willing to change; they become change agents.

THE #3 BARRIER TO EMPOWERMENT: LACK OF SELF-WORTH

John Peers observed, "You can't lead a cavalry charge if you think you look funny on a horse." Self-conscious people are rarely good leaders. They focus on themselves, worrying how they look, what others think, whether they are liked. They can't give power to others because they feel that they have no power themselves. And you can't give what you don't have.

The best leaders have a strong sense of self-worth. They believe in themselves, their mission, and their people. As author Buck Rogers says, "To those who have confidence in themselves, change is a stimulus because they believe one person can make a difference and influence what goes on around them. These people are the doers and motivators." They are also the empowerers.

Only secure leaders are able to give themselves away. Mark Twain once remarked that great things happen when you don't care who gets the credit. But I believe you can take that a step farther. I believe the greatest things happen *only* when you give others the credit. If you aspire to be a great leader, you must live by the Law of Empowerment.

DISCUSS

Answer the following questions and discuss your answers when you meet with your team.

1. *Why do some leaders violate the Law of Empowerment?*

   _____

   _____

   _____

2. *Which reason on why leaders don't share their authority is most prevalent in your profession or area of service? Give examples.*

   _____

   _____

   _____

3. How has a leader's resistance to the Law of Empowerment affected you and your teams in the past?

_____

_____

_____

4. In the past, how has a leader empowered you? What was the result?

_____

_____

_____

5. Do you agree that the only way to become indispensable is to become dispensable? Explain.

_____

_____

_____

6. Are you more likely to resist empowering others due to your desire for job security, resistance to change, lack of self-worth, or another reason? How can you get past this leadership obstacle?

_____

_____

_____

7. What are some ways you will empower others in your current position?

_____

_____

_____

APPLY

1. How would you characterize yourself in the area of self-worth? Are you confident? Do you believe you have value? Do you operate from an assumption that you have positive things to offer other people and your organization? Are you willing to take risks?

If you rate yourself low in the area of security, you will have a hard time with the Law of Empowerment. You will need to take positive steps to add value to yourself or explore why your self-worth is so low.

2. Are you someone who believes in people? Make a list of the people who work for you. If there are too many to list, then write the names of those closest to you. Next rate each person's potential—not current ability—on a scale of 1 to 10.

If the numbers are low, then your belief in people is probably not very high. Until you change that, you will have difficulty empowering others. Begin dwelling on people's positive qualities and characteristics. Look for people's greatest strengths, and envision how they could leverage those strengths to achieve significant things. Imagine what individuals could become if they made the most of their gifts and opportunities. Then help them to do so.

3. If your natural inclination is to build and hold onto your power, then you must undergo a paradigm shift to become an empowering leader. Start by selecting your best people and setting them up for success. Train them, give them resources, and then help them set accomplishable goals that will help you and the organization. Then give them the responsibility and authority to follow through. And if they fail at first, help them keep trying until they succeed. Once you experience the joy and organizational effectiveness of empowering others, you will have a hard time *not* giving your power away.

TAKE ACTION

Onetime vice presidential candidate Admiral James B. Stockdale declared, "Leadership must be based on goodwill . . . It means obvious and wholehearted commitment to helping followers . . . What we need for leaders are men of heart who are so helpful that they, in effect, do away with the need for their jobs. But leaders like that are never out of a job, never out of followers. Strange as it sounds, great leaders gain authority by giving it away."

This week, find one situation in which you can share your authority with someone else. It could be letting your child plan a family event for the weekend or giving someone on your team authority over a project. Answer the following questions throughout the week in order to evaluate the experience.

I shared my authority with _____
by empowering him or her to _____.

1. *Why did you choose this person to share your authority with?*

   _____

   _____

   _____

2. *What were you initial concerns when sharing your authority with someone else?*

   _____

   _____

   _____

3. *How did this person react to your offer?*

   _____

   _____

   _____

4. *What were some of the challenges this person faced with the project, task, or decision?*

   _____

   _____

   _____

5. *How did you encourage this person?*

_____

_____

_____

6. *How did you help the individual grow as a leader?*

_____

_____

_____

7. *What was the outcome of the project, task, or decision?*

_____

_____

_____

8. *How was sharing authority beneficial to you and to the other person?*

_____

_____

_____

13

THE LAW OF THE PICTURE

People Do What People See

GOOD LEADERS ARE ALWAYS CONSCIOUS OF THE FACT THAT THEY ARE SET-
ting the example and others are going to do what they do, for better or worse.
In general, the better the leaders' actions, the better their people's.

Several years ago, filmmaker Steven Spielberg and actor Tom Hanks produced a series
of television shows on HBO called *Band of Brothers* based on the book of the same
name by historian Stephen Ambrose. The ten episodes chronicled the story of Easy
Company, a group of paratroopers from the 101st Airborne who fought during World
War II. The men of Easy Company were as tough as soldiers get, and they fought hero-
ically from the invasion of Normandy to the end of the war.

The story of Easy Company is a great study in leadership, for the various sergeants,
lieutenants, and captains who commanded the men displayed many styles of leadership, both good and bad. When the leadership was good, it made the difference, not
only in the way the soldiers performed, but in the outcome of their battles and, ultimately, of the war.

From the very first episode of the television series, the contrasting leadership styles
were on display. Herbert Sobel, Easy Company's commanding officer during its training, was shown to be a brutal and autocratic leader with a sadistic streak. He drove the

men harder than the commander of any other company. He arbitrarily revoked passes and inflicted punishment. But judging from Ambrose's research, Sobel was even worse than he was depicted in the series.

Sobel drove the men mercilessly, which was fine, since he was preparing them for combat. But he didn't push himself the same way, being *barely* capable of passing the physical test required of paratroopers. Nor did he display the high level of competence he demanded from everyone else. Ambrose writes about an incident during training that was representative of Sobel's leadership:

> On one night exercise he [Sobel] decided to teach his men a lesson. He and Sergeant Evans went sneaking through the company position to steal rifles from sleeping men. The mission was successful; by daylight Sobel and Evans had nearly fifty rifles. With great fanfare, Evans called the company together and Sobel began to tell the men what miserable soldiers they were.[1]

What Sobel didn't realize was that the men he was berating weren't his own. He had wandered into the wrong camp and stolen the rifles belonging to Fox Company. Sobel didn't even realize his mistake until the commander of Fox Company came up with forty-five of his men.

The men who served under Sobel mocked him and undermined him. By the time Easy Company began preparations for the invasion of Normandy, many men were taking bets on which of them would shoot Sobel when they finally got into combat. Fortunately, Sobel was removed from his position as company commander and reassigned before they went into combat.

Another officer's highly incompetent leadership was depicted in an episode called "The Breaking Point." It recounted the Battle of the Bulge when the soldiers were preparing to take the town of Foy from the Germans. By then, the men of Easy Company were experienced veterans, and they were facing one of the most difficult times of the war. They suffered from bitter cold and from merciless shelling by German artillery.

During that time, an Easy Company platoon was commanded by Lieutenant Dike, a leader with political connections but no previous combat experience. Dike's method of leadership was to avoid his men, refuse to make a decision, and disappear for long periods of time to "take a walk," including when he was needed most. Not one of the men respected him. And when Dike was finally required to lead his men into an assault on the town, he failed miserably and was relieved of command.

Fortunately, most of Easy Company's leaders were excellent, and one in particular was awarded the Distinguished Service Cross and was considered by the men to be "the best combat leader in World War II."[2] That person was Dick Winters. He started out as a platoon leader in Easy Company during their training and was promoted to company commander after Normandy and then to battalion executive officer. He finished his military career with the rank of major.

Time after time, Winters helped his men to perform at the highest level. And he always led from in front, setting the example, taking the risks along with his men. Ambrose describes Winters's philosophy of leadership simply as "officers go first."[3] Whenever his troops needed to assault an enemy position, Winters was in front leading the charge.

One of the most remarkable incidents demonstrating Winters's way of leading by example occurred soon after D-Day on the road to Carentan, a town that Easy Company needed to take from the Germans. As the American paratroopers under his command approached the town, they became pinned down by German machine-gun fire. Huddled in ditches on either side of the road, they wouldn't move forward when ordered to. Yet if they didn't move, they would eventually be cut to pieces. Winters tried rallying them. He coaxed them. He kicked them. He ran from one ditch to the other as machine-gun bullets flew by. Finally, he jumped into the middle of the road, bullets glancing off the ground near him, and shouted at the men to get moving. Everyone got up and moved forward as one. And they helped to take the town.

More than thirty-five years later, Floyd Talbert, a sergeant at the time, wrote to Winters to comment about the incident: "I'll never forget seeing you in the middle of that road. You were my total inspiration. All my boys felt the same way."[4] In 2006, Winters summed up his approach to leadership, saying, "I may not have been the best combat commander, but I always strove to be. My men depended on me to carefully analyze every tactical situation, to maximize the resources that I had at my disposal, to think under pressure, and then to lead them by personal example."[5]

When Ambrose was asked what allowed Easy Company to distinguish itself during the war, to "rise above" its peers, Ambrose was clear in his response: "They weren't all that much better than other paratroopers, or the Rangers, or the Marines. They were one of many elite units in the war. But what made them special even among those who were already self-selected and special, was their leadership . . . The great COs, platoon leaders and sergeants—not all elite units had such luck in their leaders, and that's the difference."[6] Why did that make such a difference? Because people do what people see. That is the Law of the Picture. When the leaders show the way with the right actions, their followers copy them and succeed.

OBSERVE

When times are tough, uncertainty is high, and chaos threatens to overwhelm everyone, followers need a clear picture from their leaders the most. That's when they need a leader who embraces the Law of the Picture. The living picture they see in their leader produces energy, passion, and motivation to keep going.

1. *What was the major difference in leadership style between Winters, Sobel, and Dike?*

_____

_____

_____

2. *What made Winters a successful leader?*

_____

_____

_____

3. *Do you agree with the author that people do what people see? Give an example.*

_____

_____

_____

4. Describe how a leader in your organization or area of service is leading by example.

_____

_____

_____

5. According to the Law of the Picture, how do leaders direct their teams to success?

_____

_____

_____

LEARN

Great leaders always seem to embody two seemingly disparate qualities. They are both highly *visionary* and highly *practical*. Their vision enables them to see beyond the immediate. They can envision what's coming and what must be done. Leaders possess an understanding of how . . .

>   Mission provides *purpose*—answering the question, *Why?*
>   Vision provides a *picture*—answering the question, *What?*
>   Strategy provides a *plan*—answering the question, *How?*

As author Hans Finzel observed, "Leaders are paid to be dreamers. The higher you go in leadership, the more your work is about the future."

At the same time, leaders are practical enough to know that vision without action achieves nothing. They make themselves responsible for helping their followers to take action. That can be difficult because followers often cannot envision the future as the leader does. They can't picture what's best for the team. They lose track of the big picture. Why? Because vision has a tendency to leak.

Leaders are stewards of the vision. So what should they do to bridge the vision gap between them and their followers? The temptation for many leaders is to merely communicate about the vision. Don't get me wrong: communication is certainly important. Good leaders must communicate the vision clearly, creatively, and continually. The leader's effective *communication* of the vision makes the picture clear. But that is not enough. The leader must also live the vision. The leader's effective *modeling* of the vision makes the picture come alive!

That's not to say that leaders have all the answers. Anyone who has led anything knows that. The leaders who make the greatest impact are often those who lead well in the midst of uncertainty. Andy Stanley, an excellent leader and communicator, has addressed this issue. A few years ago at the Catalyst conference for leaders, he said,

> Uncertainty is not an indication of poor leadership. Rather it indicates a need for leadership. The nature of leadership demands that there always be an element of uncertainty. The temptation is to think, *If I were a good leader, I would know exactly what to do.* Increased responsibility means dealing with more and more intangibles and therefore more complex uncertainty. Leaders can afford to be uncertain, but we cannot afford to be unclear. People will not follow fuzzy leadership.

MODELING INSIGHTS FOR LEADERS

If you desire to be the best leader you can become, you must not neglect the Law of the Picture. As you strive to improve as an example to your followers, remember these things:

1. FOLLOWERS ARE ALWAYS WATCHING WHAT YOU DO

If you are a parent, you have probably already realized that your children are always watching what you do. Say anything you want, but your children learn more from what they see than from anywhere else. As parents, Margaret and I realized this early. No matter what we taught our children, they insisted on behaving like us. How frustrating. Legendary UCLA basketball coach John Wooden quotes a poem that explains it perfectly:

No written word
nor spoken plea
Can teach our youth
what they should be

Nor all the books
on all the shelves
It's what the teachers
are themselves.[7]

Just as children watch their parents and emulate their behavior, so do employees watching their bosses. If the bosses come in late, then employees feel that they can too. If the bosses cut corners, employees cut corners. People do what people see.

Followers may doubt what their leaders say, but they usually believe what they do. And they imitate it. Former U.S. Army general and secretary of state Colin Powell observed, "You can issue all the memos and give all the motivational speeches you want, but if the rest of the people in your organization don't see you putting forth your very best effort every single day, they won't either."

Whitley David asserted, "A good supervisor is a catalyst, not a drill sergeant. He creates an atmosphere where intelligent people are willing to follow him. He doesn't command; he convinces." Nothing is more convincing than living out what you say you believe.

2. It's Easier to Teach What's Right Than to Do What's Right

Writer Mark Twain quipped, "To do what is right is wonderful. To teach what is right is even more wonderful—and much easier." Isn't that the truth? It's always easier to teach what's right than it is to do it. That's one of the reasons why many parents (and bosses) say, "Do as I say, not as I do."

One of my earliest challenges as a leader was to raise my living to the level of my teaching. I can still remember the day that I decided that I would not teach anything I did not try to live out. That was a tough decision, but as a young leader, I was learning to embrace the Law of the Picture. Author Norman Vincent Peale stated, "Nothing is more confusing than people who give good advice but set a bad example." I would say a related thought is also true: "Nothing is more *convincing* than people who give good advice and set a good example."

Recently, I received calls on the same day from two reporters—one from the *Chicago Tribune* and the other from *USA Today*—about teaching ethics in the business arena. Both asked similar questions. They wanted to know if ethics could be taught. My answer was yes.

"But many of the companies that teach ethics classes had ethics problems," one reporter pushed back.

"That's because ethics can be instilled in others only if it is taught *and modeled* for them," I replied. Too many leaders are like bad travel agents. They send people places they have never been. Instead, they should be more like tour guides, taking people places they have gone and sharing the wisdom of their own experiences.

John Wooden used to say to his players, "*Show* me what you can do; don't *tell* me what you can do." I believe followers have the same attitude toward their leaders. They want to *see* their leaders in action, doing their best, showing the way, and setting the example. Featherstone remarked, "Leaders tell but never teach until they practice what they preach." That is the Law of the Picture.

3. WE SHOULD WORK ON CHANGING OURSELVES BEFORE TRYING TO IMPROVE OTHERS

Leaders are responsible for the performance of their people. The buck stops with them. They accordingly monitor their people's progress, give them direction, and hold them accountable. And to improve the performance of the team, leaders must act as change agents. However, a great danger to good leadership is the temptation to try to change others without first making changes to yourself.

As a leader, the first person I need to lead is me. The first person that I should try to change is me. My standards of excellence should be higher for myself than those I set for others. To remain a credible leader, I must always work first, hardest, and longest on changing myself. This is neither easy nor natural, but it is essential. In all honesty, I am a lot like Lucy in the *Peanuts* comic strip who tells Charlie Brown that she wants to change the world. When an overwhelmed Charlie Brown asks where she would start, her response is, "I would start with you, Charlie Brown. I would start with you."

Not long ago, I was teaching on the idea of the 360-degree leader. That is, a leader exerts his influence not just down with those he leads but also up with his boss and across with his colleagues. During a Q and A session, an attendee asked, "Which is the most difficult—leading up, across, or down?"

"None of the above," I answered quickly. "Leading myself is the toughest."

To lead any way other than by example, we send a fuzzy picture of leadership to others. If we work on improving ourselves first and make that our primary mission, then others are more likely to follow.

4. THE MOST VALUABLE GIFT A LEADER CAN GIVE IS BEING A GOOD EXAMPLE

A survey conducted by Opinion Research Corporation for Ajilon Finance asked American workers to select the one trait that was most important for a person to lead them. Here are the results:

Rank	Characteristic	Percentage
1.	Leading by example	26%
2.	Strong ethics or morals	19%
3.	Knowledge of the business	17%
4.	Fairness	14%
5.	Overall intelligence and competence	13%
6.	Recognition of employees	10%[8]

More than anything else, employees want leaders whose beliefs and actions line up. They want good models who lead from the front.

Leadership is more caught than taught. How does one "catch" leadership? By watching good leaders in action! One year in my leadership conferences, I decided to conduct an informal poll to find out what had prompted the attendees to become leaders. What I discovered did not surprise me.

10 percent became leaders because of natural gifting

5 percent became leaders as the result of a crisis

85 percent became leaders due to the influence of another leader

The overwhelming majority of leaders emerge because of the impact made on them by established leaders who modeled leadership and mentored them.

DISCUSS

Answer the following questions and discuss your answers when you meet with your team.

1. *How do vision and being practical work together in leadership?*

_____

_____

_____

2. *Explain the statement "Leaders can afford to be uncertain, but we cannot afford to be unclear."*

_____

_____

_____

3. *Give an example from your own experience of how a leader's actions have influenced you more than their words.*

_____

_____

_____

4. *How much of your time is spent on personal growth compared to the time you spend investing in your team members?*

_____

_____

_____

5. *How often do you find yourself imposing higher standards on others than you impose on yourself? How can you close the gap?*

_____

_____

_____

APPLY

1. If you are already practicing the Law of Process then you are currently working to sharpen your skills to increase your leadership ability. (If you're not, get started!) But there is more to leadership than just technical skills. Character is also vital to leadership, and that is communicated through the Law of the Picture. The primary example you set for your followers comes in the area of character, and that is the area you need to address with yourself first before trying to change others.

Give yourself a character audit. First, make a list of your core values, such as integrity, hard work, honesty, and so on. Then, think about your actions of the last month. What incidents, if any, stand out as inconsistent with those values? List as many things as you can recall. Don't dismiss anything too quickly, and don't rationalize any of them. These items will show you where you need to work on yourself. Work on changing not only your actions, but also your attitude.

2. Ask a trusted colleague or friend to watch you for an extended period of time (at least a week) to compare what you teach with how you conduct yourself. Ask him or her to record any inconsistencies. Then plan to meet at the end of the observation period to review the results. At that meeting, you may ask questions for clarification,

but you are not allowed to defend yourself. Plan to change either your actions or your philosophy to make them consistent with one another.

3. What are the three to five things you wish your people did better than they currently do now? List them. Now, grade *your performance* for each. (You may want to ask someone else to grade you as well to make sure your perception of yourself is accurate.) If your self-scores are low, then you need to change your behavior. If your scores are high, then you need to make your example more visible to your people. Adjust accordingly.

TAKE ACTION

Choose one area where you would like to see your team improve.

1. *Why do you want your team to improve in this area?*

_____

_____

_____

2. *What will success look like?*

_____

_____

_____

3. *How will you improve yourself to reach your team goal? How will you model this behavior or skill to your team? How will you get the team involved?*

_____

_____

_____

Determine a plan of action for the next few weeks or months. Set practical goals that will help to chart your progress. Remember to reward your team for reaching each goal.

14

THE LAW OF BUY-IN

People Buy into the Leader, Then the Vision

MANY PEOPLE WHO APPROACH THE AREA OF VISION IN LEADERSHIP HAVE it all backward. They believe that if the cause is good enough, people will automatically buy into it and follow. But that's not how leadership really works. People don't at first follow worthy causes. They follow worthy leaders who promote causes they can believe in. People buy into the leader first, then the leader's vision. Having an understanding of that changes your whole approach to leading people.

READ

In the fall of 1997, a few members of my staff and I had the opportunity to travel to India and teach four leadership conferences, something we've done many more times in the last decade. India is an amazing country, full of contradictions. It's a place of beauty with warm and generous people. It has a strong emerging economy. Yet at the same time millions and millions of its inhabitants live in the worst poverty imaginable. It was there that I was reminded of the Law of Buy-In.

I'll never forget when our plane landed in Delhi. Exiting the airport, I felt as if we had been transported to another planet. There were crowds everywhere. People on bicycles, in cars, on camels and elephants. People on the streets, some sleeping right on the sidewalks. Animals roamed free, no matter where we were. And everything was in motion. As we drove along the main street toward our hotel, I also noticed something else. Banners. Wherever we looked, we could see banners celebrating India's fifty years of liberty, along with huge pictures of one man: Mahatma Gandhi.

Today, people take for granted that Gandhi was a great leader. But the story of his leadership is a marvelous study in the Law of Buy-In. Mohandas K. Gandhi, called Mahatma (which means "great soul"), was educated in London. After finishing his education in law, he traveled back to India and then to South Africa. There he worked for twenty years as a barrister and political activist. And in that time he developed as a leader, fighting for the rights of Indians and other minorities who were oppressed and discriminated against by South Africa's apartheid government.

By the time he returned to India in 1914, Gandhi was very well known and highly respected among his countrymen. Over the next several years, as he led protests and strikes around the country, people rallied to him and looked to him more and more for leadership. In 1920—a mere six years after returning to India—he was elected president of the All India Home Rule League.

The most remarkable thing about Gandhi isn't that he became a leader in India, but that he was able to change the people's vision for obtaining freedom. Before he began leading them, the people used violence in an effort to achieve their goals. For years riots against the British establishment had been common. But Gandhi's vision for change in India was based on nonviolent civil disobedience. He once said, "Nonviolence is the greatest force at the disposal of mankind. It is mightier than the mightiest weapon of destruction devised by the ingenuity of man."

Gandhi challenged the people to meet oppression with peaceful disobedience and noncooperation. Even when the British military massacred more than one thousand people at Amritsar in 1919, Gandhi called the people to stand—without fighting back. Rallying everyone to his way of thinking wasn't easy. But because the people had come to buy into him as their leader, they embraced his vision. And then they followed him faithfully. He asked them not to fight, and eventually, they stopped fighting. When he called for everyone to burn foreign-made clothes and start wearing nothing but home-spun material, millions of people started doing it. When he decided that a March to the Sea to protest the Salt Act would be their rallying point for civil disobedience against the British, the nation's leaders followed him the two hundred miles to the city of Dandi, where government representatives arrested them.

Their struggle for independence was slow and painful, but Gandhi's leadership was strong enough to deliver on the promise of his vision. In 1947, India gained home rule. Because the people had bought into Gandhi, they accepted his vision. And once they had embraced the vision, they were able to carry it out. That's how the Law of Buy-In works. The leader finds the dream and then the people. The people find the leader, and then the dream.

OBSERVE

Every message that people receive is filtered through the messenger who delivers it. If you consider the messenger to be credible, then you believe the message has value. That's one reason that actors and athletes are hired as promoters of products. People often buy Nike shoes because they have bought into Michael Jordan, Tiger Woods, or Michael Vick, not necessarily because of the quality of the shoes.

1. *Why did people buy into Gandhi's vision for nonviolent protest? How had he established himself as a leader?*

   _____

   _____

   _____

2. *How do you think the people would have reacted to Gandhi's suggestion of nonviolent protest if he had not already established himself as a leader?*

   _____

   _____

   _____

3. *Whose vision have you bought into? Why?*

   _____

   _____

   _____

4. *Who in your profession or area of service seems to have the ability to rally people around their vision? What have they done to deserve such a response?*

_____

_____

_____

LEARN

You cannot separate leaders from the causes they promote. It cannot be done, no matter how hard you try. It's not an either/or proposition. The two always go together. Take a look at the following table. It shows how people react to leaders and their vision under different circumstances:

LEADER	+	VISION	=	RESULT
Don't buy in		Don't buy in		Get another leader
Don't buy in		Buy in		Get another leader
Buy in		Don't buy in		Get another vision
Buy in		Buy in		Get behind the leader

WHEN FOLLOWERS DON'T LIKE THE LEADER OR THE VISION . . .
THEY LOOK FOR ANOTHER LEADER

The only time people will follow a leader they don't like with a vision they don't believe in is when the leader has some kind of leverage. That could be something as sinister as the threat of physical violence or as basic as the ability to withhold a paycheck. If the followers have a choice in the matter, they don't follow. And even if they don't have much of a choice, they start looking for another leader to follow. This is a no-win situation for everyone involved.

WHEN FOLLOWERS DON'T LIKE THE LEADER BUT THEY DO LIKE THE
VISION . . . THEY LOOK FOR ANOTHER LEADER

You may be surprised by this. Even though people may think a cause is good, if they
don't like the leader, they will go out and find another one. That's one reason that
coaches change teams so often in professional sports. The vision for any team always
stays the same: everyone wants to win a championship. But the players don't always
believe in their leader. And when they don't, what happens? The owners don't fire all
of the players. They fire the leader and bring in someone they hope the players will buy
into. The talent level of most professional coaches is similar. The effectiveness of their
systems isn't much different. What often separates them is their leadership and the level
of credibility with their players.

WHEN FOLLOWERS LIKE THE LEADER BUT NOT THE VISION . . .
THEY CHANGE THE VISION

When followers don't agree with their leader's vision, they react in many ways.
Sometimes they work to convince their leader to change the vision. Sometimes they
abandon their point of view and adopt their leader's. Other times they find a compro-
mise. But as long as they still buy into the leader, they rarely out-and-out reject him.
They will keep following.

An excellent example occurred in Great Britain. Tony Blair had a long tenure in
office as prime minister. He was a popular leader, elected to serve three times. Yet at
the same time, the majority of people in Great Britain were against Blair's policy of
involving the nation in the war with Iraq. Why did Blair remain in office so long?
Because they had bought into him as a leader. As a result, they were willing to live with
their philosophical difference with him.

WHEN FOLLOWERS LIKE THE LEADER AND THE VISION . . . THEY GET
BEHIND BOTH

When people believe in their leader and the vision, they will follow their leader no
matter how bad conditions get or how much the odds are stacked against them. That's
why the Indian people in Gandhi's day refused to fight back as soldiers mowed them
down. That's what inspired the U.S. space program to fulfill John F. Kennedy's vision

and put a man on the moon. That's the reason people continued to have hope and keep alive the dream of Martin Luther King Jr., even after he was gunned down. That's what continues to inspire followers to keep running the race, even when they feel they've hit the wall and given everything they've got.

As a leader, having a great vision and a worthy cause is not enough to get people to follow you. You have to become a better leader; you must get your people to buy into you. That is the price you have to pay if you want your vision to have a chance of becoming a reality. You cannot ignore the Law of Buy-In and remain successful as a leader.

DISCUSS

Answer the following questions and discuss your answers when you meet with your team.

1. *How do leaders and followers differ when it comes to supporting a vision?*

_____

_____

_____

2. *Under what circumstances would a follower look for another leader?*

_____

_____

_____

3. *Why might you stay with a leader whose vision began to depart from what it was when you began following him or her?*

_____

_____

_____

4. *Do you agree with the author that, "The leader finds the dream and then the people. The people find the leader and then the dream"? Explain.*

_____

_____

_____

5. *Have you ever cast vision and not had people buy into it and follow? How might your leadership have affected the response you received? Explain.*

_____

_____

_____

6. *Up to now, did you approach leadership with the understanding that people must first buy into you before they will buy into you vision? Give an example of your previous leadership approach to casting vision and rallying followers.*

_____

_____

_____

APPLY

1. Do you have a vision for your leadership and your organization? Why do you lead? What are you trying to accomplish? Write your thoughts in a vision statement. Is that vision worthy of your time and effort? Is it something you're willing to give a significant portion of your life to? (If not, rethink what you are doing and why.)

2. What is the level of buy-in for the people you lead? If your team is small, list all of its members. If it is large, list the key players who influence the team. Now rate each person's buy-in on a scale of 1 to 10. (A 1 means they won't even follow you in areas where they are required to according to their job description. A 10 means they would follow you into battle even in the face of death.) If your people don't buy into you,

they will not help you execute your vision—even if they love it. They will find a new leader to lead them.

3. Think about ways you can earn credibility with each person. There are many ways you can do that:

- By developing a good relationship with him
- By being honest and authentic and developing trust
- By holding yourself to high standards and setting a good example
- By giving him the tools to do his job better
- By helping him to achieve his personal goals
- By developing him as a leader

Develop a strategy with each person. If you make it your primary goal to add value to all of them, your credibility factor will rise rapidly.

TAKE ACTION

As a leader you don't earn any points for failing in a noble cause. You don't get credit for being "right." Your success is measured by your ability to actually take the people where they need to go. But you can do that only if the people first buy into you as a leader.

Think about some problem, project or goal that you have a vision for. Then think about who could help you to realize that vision. During the coming weeks, intentionally build relationships with those people, and do what you can to help them be successful. Only after you have invested in them should you share your vision. Once you have, note how they respond.

Vision: _____

Person who can help me realize my vision: _____

I will intentionally build a relationship with this person by:

_____

_____

_____

Ways I can add value to him or her:

1. _____

_____

2. _____

_____

3. _____

_____

The level of my connection before I shared my vision was _____.

How this person responded to my vision:

_____

_____

_____

15

THE LAW OF VICTORY

Leaders Find a Way for the Team to Win

Have you ever thought about what separates the leaders who achieve victory from those who suffer defeat? What does it take to make a team a winner? It's hard to identify the quality that separates winners from losers. Every leadership situation is different. Every crisis has its own challenges. But I think that victorious leaders have one thing in common: they share an unwillingness to accept defeat. The alternative to winning is totally unacceptable to them. As a result, they figure out what must be done to achieve victory.

READ

Crisis seems to bring out the best—and the worst—in leaders because at such times the pressure is intense and the stakes are high. That was certainly true during World War II when Adolf Hitler was threatening to crush Europe and remake it according to his vision. But against the power of Hitler and his Nazi hordes stood a leader determined to win, a practitioner of the Law of Victory: British Prime Minister Winston Churchill. He inspired the British people to resist Hitler and ultimately win the war.

Long before he became prime minister in 1940, Churchill spoke out against the Nazis. He seemed like the lone critic in 1932 when he warned, "Do not delude yourselves . . . Do not believe that all Germany is asking for is equal status . . . They are looking for weapons and when they have them believe me they will ask for the return of lost territories or colonies." As a leader, Churchill could see what was coming, and he was trying to prepare the people of England for what he saw as an inevitable fight.

In successive years, Churchill continued to speak out against the Nazis. And when Hitler annexed Austria in 1938, Churchill said to members of the House of Commons:

> For five years I have talked to the House on these matters—not with very great success. I have watched this famous island descending incontinently, fecklessly, the stairway which leads to a dark gulf . . . Now is the time at last to rouse the nation. Perhaps it is the last time it can be roused with a chance of preventing war, or with a chance of coming through with victory should our effort to prevent war fail.[1]

Unfortunately, Prime Minister Neville Chamberlain and the other leaders of Great Britain did not make a stand against Hitler. They were not prepared to do what it took to achieve victory. And more of Europe fell to the Nazis.

By mid-1940, most of Europe was under Germany's thumb. But then something happened that probably changed the course of history for the free world. The leadership of England fell to the sixty-five-year-old Winston Churchill, a courageous leader who had practiced the Law of Victory throughout his life. He refused to buckle under the Nazis' threats. For more than a year, Great Britain stood alone facing the threat of German invasion. When Hitler indicated that he wanted to make a deal with England, Churchill defied him. When Germany began bombing England, the British stood strong. And all the while, Churchill looked for a way to gain victory.

Time after time, Churchill rallied the British people. It began with his first speech after becoming prime minister:

> We have before us an ordeal of the most grievous kind. We have before us many, many long months of struggle and of suffering. You ask, what is our policy? I can say: It is to wage war, by sea, land and air, with all our might and with all the strength that God can give us; to wage war against a monstrous tyranny, never surpassed in the dark, lamentable catalogue of human crime. That is our policy. You ask, what is our aim? I can answer in one word: Victory—victory at all costs, victory in spite of all terror, victory, however long and hard the road may be; for without victory, there is no survival.[2]

Meanwhile, Churchill did everything in his power to prevail. He deployed troops in the Mediterranean against Mussolini's forces. Although he hated communism, he allied himself with Stalin and the Soviets, sending them aid even when Great Britain's supplies were threatened and its survival hung in the balance. And he developed his personal relationship with another powerful leader: Franklin Roosevelt. Though the president of the United States was reluctant to enter the war, Churchill worked to build a relationship with him, hoping to change it from one of friendship and mutual respect to a full-fledged war alliance. In time his efforts paid off. On the day the Japanese bombed Pearl Harbor, ushering the United States into the war, Churchill is said to have remarked to himself, "So we have won after all."

When Churchill sought the aid of Franklin Roosevelt, he was enlisting a leader who had practiced the Law of Victory for decades. It was a hallmark of Roosevelt's entire life. He had found a way to achieve political victory while winning over polio. When he was elected president and became responsible for pulling the American people out of the Great Depression, it was just another impossible situation that he learned how to fight through. And fight he did. Through the 1930s, the country was slowly recovering due in large part to his leadership.

The stakes during the war were undoubtedly high. Pulitzer Prize–winning historian Arthur Schlesinger Jr. noted, "The Second World War found democracy fighting for its life. By 1941, there were only a dozen or so democratic states left on earth. But great leadership emerged in time to rally the democratic cause." The team of Roosevelt and Churchill provided that leadership like a one-two punch. Just as the prime minister had rallied England, the president brought together the American people and united them in a common cause as no one ever had before or has since.

To Churchill and Roosevelt, victory was the only option. If they had accepted anything less, the world would be a very different place today. Schlesinger stated, "Take a look at our present world. It is manifestly not Adolf Hitler's world. His Thousand-Year Reich turned out to have a brief and bloody run of a dozen years. It is manifestly not Joseph Stalin's world. That ghastly world self-destructed before our eyes."[3] Without Churchill and England, all of Europe would have fallen. Without Roosevelt and the United States, it might never have been reclaimed for freedom. But not even an Adolf Hitler and the army of the Third Reich could stand against two leaders dedicated to the Law of Victory.

OBSERVE

When the pressure is on, great leaders are at their best. Whatever is inside them comes to the surface and works for or against them.

1. *How do the words of Winston Churchill reflect the Law of Victory?*

   _____

   _____

   _____

2. *How do the actions of Winston Churchill reflect the Law of Victory?*

   _____

   _____

   _____

3. *How do you think Franklin Roosevelt's prior commitment to the Law of Victory factored into how he led America during WWII?*

   _____

   _____

   _____

4. *Identify and describe someone in your profession or area of service who reflects the Law of Victory.*

   _____

   _____

   _____

LEARN

Whether it's a sports team, an army, a business, or a nonprofit organization, victory is possible as long as you have three components that contribute to a team's dedication to victory.

1. Unity of Vision

Teams succeed only when the players have a unified vision, no matter how much talent or potential there is. A team doesn't win the championship if its players are working from different agendas. That's true in professional sports. That's true in business. That's true in nonprofits.

I learned this lesson in high school when I was a junior on the varsity basketball team. We had a very talented group of kids, and many people had picked us to win the state championship. But we had a problem. The juniors and seniors on the team refused to work together. It got so bad that the coach eventually gave up trying to get us to play together and divided us into two different squads for our games, one comprised of seniors, the other comprised of juniors. In the end the team had miserable results. Why? We didn't share a common vision. People played for their fellow classmen, not the team.

2. Diversity of Skills

It almost goes without saying that a team needs diversity in skills. Can you imagine a whole hockey team of goalies? Or a football team of quarterbacks? How about a business where there are *only* salespeople or nothing but accountants? Or a nonprofit organization with just fund-raisers? Or only strategists? It doesn't make sense. Every organization requires diverse talents to succeed.

Some leaders have blind spots in this area. In fact, I used to be one of them. I'm embarrassed to say there was a time in my life when I thought that if people would just be more like me, they would be successful. I'm wiser now and understand that every person has something to contribute. We're all like parts of the human body. For that body to do its best, it needs *all* of its parts, each doing its own job.

I recognize how each person on my team contributes using his or her unique skills, and I express my appreciation for them. The newer you are to leadership and the stronger your natural leadership ability, the more likely you will be to overlook the importance of others on the team. Don't fall into that trap.

3. A Leader Dedicated to Victory and Raising Players to Their Potential

It's true that having good players with diverse skills is important. As former Notre Dame head football coach Lou Holtz says, "You've got to have great athletes to win, I don't care who the coach is. You can't win without good athletes, but you can lose with them. This is where coaching makes the difference." In other words, you also require leadership to achieve victory.

Unity of vision doesn't happen spontaneously. The right players with the proper diversity of talent don't come together on their own. It takes a leader to make those things happen. It takes a leader to provide the motivation, empowerment, and direction required to win.

DISCUSS

Answer the following questions and discuss your answers when you meet with your team.

1. What are the three components that the author believes are necessary for victory?

_____

_____

_____

2. Are there other factors the author didn't mention? If so, name them.

_____

_____

_____

3. *Has anyone in your organization consistently demonstrated the Law of Victory?*

_____

_____

_____

4. *Which of the three components of victory do you think your team strongly displays? Explain.*

_____

_____

_____

5. *How can your team strengthen its Unity of Vision?*

_____

_____

_____

6. *As a leader, how can you express your dedication to victory?*

_____

_____

_____

APPLY

1. The first step in practicing the Law of Victory is taking responsibility for the success of the team, department, or organization you lead. It must become *personal.* Your commitment must be higher than that of your team members. Your passion should be high. Your dedication must be unquestioned.

Do you currently demonstrate that kind of commitment? If not, you need to examine yourself to determine if it is in you. If you search yourself and are unable to convince yourself to bring that kind of commitment, then one of three things is probably true:

- You are pursing the wrong vision.
- You are in the wrong organization.
- You are not the right leader for the job.

You will have to make adjustments accordingly.

2. If you are dedicated to leading your team to victory, you will be able to achieve it only if you have the right people on the team. Think about all the skills necessary to achieve your goals. Write them down. Now compare that list with the names of the people on your team. If there are functions or tasks for which no one on the team is suited, you need to add members to the team or train the ones you have.

3. The other crucial component for leading your team to victory is unity of vision. Do a little informal research to find out what's important to your team members. Ask them what they want to achieve personally. And ask them to describe the purpose or mission of the team, department, or organization. If you get a diversity of answers, you need to work on communicating a single vision clearly, creatively, and continually until everyone is on the same page. You should also work with each team member to show how personal goals can align with the team's overall goals.

TAKE ACTION

You and each person on your team have a unique set of gifts, talents, and training. This week, if your team has not already, take a personality test such as DISC or Myers Briggs. Then have each person, including yourself, fill out the survey below. Individually review each person's test and survey answers and discuss with him or her the part he or she plays on the team. Also, let the team know about opportunities that are available to them to improve or learn specific skills.

1. *What job task do you enjoy doing the most? Why?*

_____

_____

_____

2. *What job task do you least enjoy? Why?*

_____

_____

_____

3. *What are your hobbies and interests?*

_____

_____

_____

4. *What is your formal training? (degrees, certifications, classes taken)*

_____

_____

_____

5. *Outside of your obvious job skills, what other skills or training do you have?*

_____

_____

_____

16

THE LAW OF THE BIG MO

Momentum Is a Leader's Best Friend

I F YOU'VE GOT ALL THE PASSION, TOOLS, AND PEOPLE YOU NEED TO FULFILL a great vision, yet you can't seem to get your organization moving and going in the right direction, you're dead in the water as a leader. If you can't get things going, you will not succeed. What do you need in such circumstances? You need to look to the Law of the Big Mo and harness the power of the leader's best friend: momentum.

READ

Several years ago I saw a movie called *Stand and Deliver* that illustrates the hopelessness many people feel in an organization without momentum. Maybe you've seen it too. It's about a real-life teacher named Jaime Escalante who worked at Garfield High School in East Los Angeles, California.

Teaching, motivating, and leading were in Jaime Escalante's blood, even from the time of his youth in his native La Paz, Bolivia. He quickly became known as his city's finest teacher. When he was in his thirties, Escalante and his family immigrated to the United States. He worked several years in a restaurant, and then at Russell Electronics. Though he could have pursued a promising career at Russell, he went back to school and earned a second bachelor's degree so that he could teach in the United States. Escalante's burning desire was to make a difference in people's lives.

At age forty-three, he was hired by Garfield High School to teach computer science.

But when he arrived at Garfield on the first day of class, he found that there was no funding for computers. And because his degree was in mathematics, he would be teaching basic math. Disappointed, he went in search of his first class, hoping that his dream of making a difference wasn't slipping through his fingers.

The change from computers to math turned out to be the least of Escalante's problems. The school, which had been empty and quiet during his summertime interview, was now in chaos. Discipline was nonexistent. Fights seemed to break out continually. Trash and graffiti were everywhere. Students—and even outsiders from the neighborhood—roamed all over the campus throughout the day. Gang activity was rampant. It was a teacher's worst nightmare.

Almost daily he thought of quitting. But his passion for teaching and his dedication to improving the lives of his students wouldn't allow him to give up. Yet at the same time Escalante was enough of a leader to know that the students were doomed if the school didn't change. They were all sliding backward fast, and they needed something to move them forward.

When a new principal was brought in, things began to change for the better. But Escalante wanted to take it further. He believed that the way to improve the school was to challenge the school's best and brightest with a calculus class that would prepare them for an AP class earning them college credit. A few AP tests were already being given on campus in Spanish. Occasionally, an individual student would attempt a test in physics or history. But the problem was that the school didn't have a leader with vision to take up the cause. That's where Escalante came into play.

In the fall of 1978, Escalante organized the first calculus class. Rounding up every possible candidate who might be able to handle the course from Garfield's 3,500 student population, he was able to find only 14 students. In the first few classes, he laid out the work it would take for them to prepare for the AP calculus test at the end of the year. By the end of the second week of school, he had lost 7 students. Even the ones who stayed were not well prepared for calculus. And by late spring, he was down to only 5 students. All of them took the AP test in May, but only 2 passed.

Escalante was disappointed, but he refused to give up, especially since he had made progress. He knew that if he could help his students experience a few wins, build their confidence, and give them hope, he could move them forward. He was determined to do whatever it took. To motivate them, he'd give them extra homework or challenge one of the school's athletes to a handball match. (Escalante never lost!) If they needed encouragement, he'd take them out to McDonald's as a reward. If they got lazy, he'd inspire, amaze, amuse, and even intimidate them. And all along the way, he modeled hard work, dedication to excellence, and what he called *ganas*—desire.

The next fall, Escalante put together another calculus class, this time with nine students. At the end of the year, eight took the test and six passed. He was making progress. Word of his success spread. Students heard that Escalante's protégés were earning college credit, and in the fall of 1980, his calculus class numbered fifteen. When they all took the test at the end of the year, fourteen students passed. The steps forward weren't huge, but Escalante could see that the program was building momentum.

The next group of students, numbering eighteen, was the subject of the movie *Stand and Deliver*. Like their predecessors, they worked very hard to learn calculus, many coming to school at 7:00 a.m. every day—a full hour and a half before school started. And often they stayed until 5:00, 6:00, or 7:00 p.m. And though Educational Testing Service (ETS) questioned the validity of the first test the students took and they had to take it a second time, 100 percent of them passed.

After that, the math program exploded. In 1983, the number of students passing the AP calculus exam almost doubled, from 18 to 31. The next year it doubled again, the number reaching 63. And it continued growing. In 1987, 129 students took the test, with 85 of them receiving college credit. Garfield High School in East Los Angeles, once considered the sinkhole of the district, produced 27 percent of all passing AP calculus test scores by Mexican-Americans in the entire United States.

The benefits of the Law of the Big Mo were felt by all of Garfield High School's students. The school started offering classes to prepare students for other AP exams. In time, Garfield held regular AP classes in Spanish, calculus, history, European history, biology, physics, French, government, and computer science.

In 1987, nine years after Escalante spearheaded the program, Garfield students took more than 325 AP examinations. Most incredibly, Garfield had a waiting list of more than 400 students from areas outside its boundaries wanting to enroll. The school that was once the laughingstock of the district and that had almost lost its accreditation had become one of the top three inner-city schools in the entire nation![1] That's the power of the Law of the Big Mo.

OBSERVE

Momentum really is a leader's best friend because many times it's the only thing that makes the difference between losing and winning. When you have no momentum, even the simplest tasks seem impossible. Small problems look like insurmountable obstacles. Morale becomes low. The future appears dark. An organization with no momentum is like a train at a dead stop. It's hard to get going, and even small wooden blocks on the track can keep it from going anywhere.

On the other hand, when you have momentum on your side, the future looks bright, obstacles appear small, and troubles seem inconsequential. An organization with momentum is like a train that's moving at sixty miles per hour. You could build a steel-reinforced concrete wall across the tracks, and the train would plow right through it.

1. *What obstacles did Escalante face at Garfield High School?*

_____

_____

_____

2. *How did he create the momentum needed for the students to succeed and to grow the AP program?*

_____

_____

_____

3. *How did the student body, not just those in his class, benefit from his actions?*

_____

_____

_____

4. What do you think would have happened if the eighteen students hadn't retaken the test?

_____

_____

_____

5. Is your organization or department currently experiencing positive momentum?

_____

_____

_____

6. What obstacles to momentum are you currently facing?

_____

_____

_____

7. What will it take to overcome them?

_____

_____

_____

LEARN

If you want your organization, department, or team to succeed, you must learn the Law of Momentum and make the most of it in your organization. Here are some things about momentum that you need to know:

1. MOMENTUM IS THE GREAT EXAGGERATOR

The Law of the Big Mo at work is easily seen in sports because the swings in momentum occur in the space of a few hours right before your eyes. When a team gets on a roll, every play seems to work. Every shot seems to score. The team seems to do no wrong. The opposite is also true. When a team is in a slump, no matter how hard you work or how many solutions you try, nothing seems to work. Momentum is like a magnifying glass; it makes things look bigger than they really are. That's why I call it the great exaggerator. And it's one reason that leaders work so hard to control momentum.

Because momentum has such a great impact, leaders try to control it. That's why in basketball games, for instance, when the opposing team is scoring a lot of unanswered points and starts to develop momentum, a good coach will call a time-out. Why? He's trying to stop the other team's momentum before it becomes too strong. If he doesn't, his team will likely lose the game.

When was the last time you heard of a team on the cusp of winning a championship complain about injuries? Or second-guess the team's ability? Or totally rethink strategy? It doesn't happen. Is that because no one is injured and everything is perfect? No. It's because success is exaggerated by momentum. When you have momentum, you don't worry about small problems, and many larger ones seem to work themselves out.

2. Momentum Makes Leaders Look Better Than They Are

When leaders have momentum on their side, people think they're geniuses. They look past shortcomings. They forget about the mistakes the leaders have made. Momentum changes everyone's perspective of leaders. People like associating themselves with winners.

Young leaders often get less credit than they deserve. I often encourage young leaders just not to lose heart. When leaders are new in their careers, they don't have any momentum yet, and others often don't give them any credit. Experienced leaders think the younger ones don't know anything.

Once a leader creates some success for his organization and develops career momentum, then people give him *more* credit than he deserves. Why? Because of the Law of the Big Mo. Momentum exaggerates a leader's success and makes him look better than he really is. It may not seem fair, but that's just the way it works.

For many years I have tried to add value to people. After writing fifty books and hundreds of lesson on leadership and success, I have gained a lot of momentum. Everything I do to add value to people seems to be compounding in a positive way. Often I say that when I started my career, I wasn't as bad as people thought. Today, I'm not as good as people give me credit for. Why the difference? Momentum!

3. Momentum Helps Followers Perform Better Than They Are

When leadership is strong and there is momentum in an organization, people are motivated and inspired to perform at higher levels. They become effective beyond their hopes and expectations. If you remember the 1980 U.S. Olympic hockey team, you know what I'm talking about. The team was good, but not good enough to win the gold medal. Yet that's what the Americans did. Why? Because leading up to the championship game, they won game after game against very tough teams. They gained so much momentum that they performed beyond everyone's expectations. And after they beat the Russians, nothing could stop them from coming home with the gold medal.

The same kind of thing is true in business and volunteer organizations. When an organization has great momentum, all participants are more successful than they would be otherwise. I'll tell you how you know that's true. If you see leaders (especially mid-level ones) who had great success in an organization with momentum leave that organization and suddenly their performance becomes merely average, you know the Law of the Big Mo was at work. Even average people can perform far above average in an organization with great momentum.

4. Momentum Is Easier to Steer Than to Start

Have you ever been waterskiing? If you have, you know that it's harder to get up on the water than it is to steer once you're up there. Think about the first time you skied. Before you got up, the boat was dragging you along, and you probably thought your arms were going to give way as the water flooded against your chest and into your face. For a moment, you might have believed you couldn't hold on to the tow rope any longer. But then the force of the water drove your skis onto the surface, and off you went. At that point, you were able to make a turn with only a subtle shift of weight from one foot to another. That's the way the momentum of leadership works. Getting started is a struggle, but once you're moving forward, you can really start to do some amazing things.

5. Momentum Is the Most Powerful Change Agent

Given enough momentum, nearly any kind of change is possible in an organization. People like to get on a winning bandwagon. Followers trust leaders with a proven track record. They accept changes from people who have led them to victory before. Momentum puts victory within reach.

6. MOMENTUM IS THE LEADER'S RESPONSIBILITY

It takes a leader to create momentum. Followers can catch it. Good managers are able to use it to their advantage once it has begun. Everyone can enjoy the benefits it brings. But *creating* momentum requires someone who has vision, can assemble a good team, and motivates others. If the leader is looking for someone to motivate him, then the organization is in trouble. If the leader is waiting for the organization to develop momentum on its own, then the organization is in trouble. It is the leader's responsibility to initiate momentum and keep it going. U.S.

7. MOMENTUM BEGINS INSIDE THE LEADER

Momentum begins within the individual leader. It starts with vision, passion, and enthusiasm. It starts with energy. Inspirational writer Eleanor Doan observed, "You cannot kindle a fire in any other heart until it is burning within your own."

If you don't believe in the vision and enthusiastically pursue it, doing all that you can to bring it to fruition, then you won't start making the small gains required to get the ball rolling. However, if you model enthusiasm to your people day in and day out, you attract like-minded people to your team, department, or organization, and motivate them to achieve. You will begin to see forward progress. Once you do, you will begin to generate momentum. And if you're wise, you'll value it for what it is: the leader's best friend. Once you have it, you can do almost anything. That's the power of the Big Mo.

DISCUSS

Answer the following questions and discuss your answers when you meet with your team.

1. *How do leaders benefit from momentum?*

_____

_____

_____

2. *How do followers benefit from momentum?*

_____

_____

_____

3. *Do you agree with the author that "with momentum nearly any kind of change is possible"? Explain.*

_____

_____

_____

4. *Describe the momentum in your organization.*

_____

_____

_____

5. *Who are the momentum makers in your organization? What have they done recently to create momentum?*

_____

_____

_____

6. *What would create additional momentum in the organization?*

_____

_____

_____

7. What are you doing to become a momentum maker?

_____

_____

_____

APPLY

1. Momentum begins inside the leader and spreads from there. Have you taken responsibility for the momentum in the area of which you are the leader? Are you passionate about the vision? Do you display enthusiasm at all times? Do you work to motivate others even when you don't feel like it? You must model the attitude and work ethic that you would like to see in others. That often requires what I call character leadership.

2. Motivation is a key factor in developing momentum. The first step toward building motivation is removing demotivating elements within the organization. What in your area of responsibility is causing people to lose their passion and enthusiasm? How can you go about removing or at least minimizing those factors? Once you have done that, you can then take the next step, which is to identify and put into play specific elements that will motivate your followers.

3. To encourage momentum, you need to help your people celebrate their accomplishments. Make it a regular practice to honor people who "move the ball forward." You want to continually praise effort, but *reward* accomplishments. The more you reward success, the more people will strive for it.

TAKE ACTION

President Harry Truman once said, "If you can't stand the heat, get out of the kitchen." But for leaders, that statement should be changed to, "If you can't *make* some heat, get out of the kitchen."

As the leader you need to look for ways your team can experience wins by accomplishing goals. First start with the smaller things you know they can achieve and gradually move them to larger goals that are more difficult. These accomplishments will build team momentum and allow your team to attempt and accomplish even more.

List the wins that your team will go after below. Start with the small goals and gradually move to larger goals. Be sure to celebrate each accomplishment as you achieve it to build morale.

Goals

1. _____
_____
_____

2. _____
_____
_____

3. _____
_____
_____

4. _____
_____
_____

5. _____
_____
_____

17

THE LAW OF PRIORITIES

Leaders Understand That Activity
Is Not Necessarily Accomplishment

L EADERS NEVER ADVANCE TO A POINT WHERE THEY NO LONGER NEED TO prioritize. It's something that good leaders keep doing, whether they're leading a billion-dollar corporation, running a small business, pastoring a church, coaching a team, or leading a small group. I think good leaders intuitively know that to be true.

READ

Examine the lives of all effective leaders, and you will see them putting priorities into action. Every time Norman Schwarzkopf assumed a new command, he didn't just rely on his leadership intuition; he also reexamined the unit's priorities. Lance Armstrong was able to win seven Tour de France championships because his priorities guided his training regimen. When explorer Ronald Amundsen succeeded in taking his team to the South Pole and back, it was due, in part, to his ability to set the right priorities.

Successful leaders live according to the Law of Priorities. They recognize that activity is not necessarily accomplishment. But the best leaders seem to be able to get the Law of Priorities to work for them by satisfying multiple priorities with each activity. This actually enables them to increase their focus while reducing their number of actions.

A leader who was a master at that was one of my idols: John Wooden, the former head basketball coach of the UCLA Bruins. He is called the Wizard of Westwood because the amazing feats he accomplished in the world of college sports were so incredible that they seemed to be magical.

Evidence of Wooden's ability to make the Law of Priorities work for him could be seen in the way he approached basketball practice. Wooden claimed that he learned some of his methods from watching Frank Leahy, the great former Notre Dame head football coach. He said, "I often went to his [Leahy's] practices and observed how he broke them up into periods. Then I would go home and analyze why he did things certain ways. As a player, I realized there was a great deal of time wasted. Leahy's concepts reinforced my ideas and helped in the ultimate development of what I do now."

People who have served in the military say that they often have to hurry up and wait. That seems to be true in sports too. Coaches ask their players to work their hearts out one minute and then to stand around doing nothing the next. But that's not the way Wooden worked. He orchestrated every moment of practice and planned each activity with specific purposes in mind. He employed economy of motion. Here's how he worked.

Every year, Wooden determined a list of overall priorities for the team, based on observations from the previous season. Those items might include objectives such as, "Build confidence in Drollinger and Irgovich," or "Use 3 on 2 continuity drill at least three times a week." Usually, he had about a dozen or so items that he wanted to work on throughout the season. But Wooden also reviewed his agenda for his teams every day. Each morning, he and an assistant meticulously planned the day's practice. They usually spent two hours strategizing for a practice that might not even last that long. He drew ideas from notes jotted on three-by-five cards that he always carried with him. He planned every drill, minute by minute, and recorded the information in a notebook prior to practice. Wooden once boasted that if you asked what his team was doing on a specific date at three o'clock in 1963, he could tell you precisely what drill his team was running. Like all good leaders, Wooden did the work of thinking ahead for his team.

Wooden always maintained his focus, and he found ways for his players to do the same thing. His special talent was for addressing several priority areas at once. For example, to help players work on their free throws—something that many of them found tedious—Wooden instituted a free-throw shooting policy during scrimmages that would encourage them to concentrate and improve instead of just marking the time.

The sooner a sidelined player made a set number of free throws, the sooner he could get back into action. And Wooden continually changed the number of shots required of the guards, forwards, and centers so that team members rotated in and out at different rates. That way everyone, regardless of position or starting status, got experience playing together, a critical priority for Wooden's development of total teamwork.

The most remarkable aspect about John Wooden—and the most telling about his ability to focus on his priorities—is that he never scouted opposing teams. Instead, he focused on getting his players to reach *their* potential. And he addressed those things through practice and personal interaction with the players. It was never his goal to win championships or even to beat the other team. His desire was to get each person to play to his potential and to put the best possible team on the floor. And of course, Wooden's results were incredible. In more than forty years of coaching, he had only *one* losing season—his first. And he led his UCLA teams to four undefeated seasons and a record ten NCAA championships.[1] No other college team has ever come close. Wooden was a great leader. He just might be the finest person to coach in any sport. Why? Because every day he lived by the Law of Priorities.

OBSERVE

Not every leader practices the discipline of prioritizing. Why? I believe there are a few reasons. First, when we are busy, we naturally believe that we are achieving. But busyness does not equal productivity. Activity is not necessarily accomplishment. Second, prioritizing requires leaders to continually think ahead, to know what's important, to know what's next, to see how everything relates to the overall vision. That's hard work. Third, prioritizing causes us to do things that are at the least uncomfortable and sometimes downright painful.

1. What did Wooden do to prepare for a team practice?

_____

_____

_____

2. *Why do you think Wooden was disinterested in scouting other teams?*

_____

_____

_____

3. *Give an example of how "activity is not necessarily accomplishment."*

_____

_____

_____

4. *How do you prepare so that you can maximize your effort?*

_____

_____

_____

5. *Who in your organization or profession always seems to be "on track" with the right priorities? To what do you attribute that ability?*

_____

_____

_____

LEARN

Leaders can't afford to just think inside the box. Sometimes they need to reinvent the box—or blow it up. Executive and author Max Depree says, "The first responsibility of a leader is to define reality." That requires the Law of Priorities. When you're the leader, everything is on the table.

Every year I spend about two weeks in December reevaluating my priorities. I review the previous year's schedule. I look at my upcoming commitments. I evaluate my family life. I think about my goals. I look at the big picture of what I'm doing to make sure the way I'm living lines up with my values and priorities.

One of the guiding principles I use during this process is the Pareto Principle. I've often taught it to people at leadership conferences over the years, and I also explain it in depth in my book *Developing the Leader Within You*. The idea is this: if you focus your attention on the activities that rank in the top 20 percent in terms of importance, you will have an 80 percent return on your effort. For example, if you have ten employees, you should give 80 percent of your time and attention to the best two. If you have one hundred customers, the top twenty will provide you with 80 percent of your business, so focus on them. If your to-do list has ten items on it, the two most important ones will give you an 80 percent return on your time. If you haven't already observed this phenomenon, test it and you'll see that it really plays out that way. One year as I went through this process, I realized that I had to totally refocus and restructure one of my organizations.

The other guideline I use whenever I evaluate my priorities is the three Rs. No, not reading, writing, and 'rithmetic. My three Rs are requirement, return, and reward. I believe that to be effective, leaders must order their lives according to these three questions:

1. WHAT IS REQUIRED?

We're all accountable to somebody for the work we do—an employer, a board of directors, stockholders, the government, and so on. We also have responsibility for the important people in our lives, such as spouse, children, and parents. For that reason, any list of priorities must begin with what is required of us.

The question I ask myself is, *What must I do that nobody can or should do for me?* As I have gotten older, that list has gotten shorter and shorter. If I'm doing something that's not necessary, I should eliminate it. If I'm doing something that's necessary but not required of me personally, I need to delegate it.

2. WHAT GIVES THE GREATEST RETURN?

As a leader, you should spend most of your time working in your areas of greatest strength. Marcus Buckingham and Donald O. Clifton have done extensive research on this subject, which you can read about in their book *Now, Discover Your Strengths*. People are more productive and more content when their work is within their natural gifting and strengths. Ideally, leaders should get out of their comfort zone but stay in their strength zone.

What's the practical application for this? Here's my rule of thumb. If something I'm doing can be done 80 percent as well by someone else, I delegate it. If you have a responsibility that someone else could do according to that standard—or that could *potentially* meet that standard—then develop and train a person to handle it. Just because you *can* do something does not mean that you *should* do it. Remember, leaders understand that activity is not necessarily accomplishment. That's the Law of Priorities.

3. What Brings the Greatest Reward?

This final question relates to personal satisfaction. Tim Redmond, president of Redmond Leadership Institute, observed, "There are many things that will catch my eye, but there are only a few things that will catch my heart."

Life is too short not to do some things you love. I love teaching leadership. I love writing and speaking. I love spending time with my wife, children, and grandchildren. I love playing golf. No matter what else I do, I will make time for those things. They are the fire lighters in my life. They energize me and keep me passionate. And passion provides the fuel in a person's life to keep him going.

REORDERING PRIORITIES

A few years ago when I went through this process of reprioritizing, I revisited the way I was spending my time. Back when I wrote the first edition of this book, I determined to spend my work time according to the following guideline:

Area	Time Allotted
Leadership	19 percent
Communicating	38 percent
Creating	31 percent
Networking	12 percent

These four areas represent my greatest strengths. They are the most rewarding aspects of my career. And they are also aligned with my responsibilities to my companies.

I realized as I was reviewing these areas that I was not maintaining the balance I desired. I was spending too much time in hands-on leadership at one of my companies, and it was taking away from higher priorities. Once again, I had to recognize that activity is not necessarily accomplishment. I knew I was in for another difficult business decision. If I was going to continue to be effective in fulfilling my vision, I would have to change and work according to the Law of Priorities. I made the decision to sell one of my companies. It wasn't easy, but it was the right thing for me to do.

DISCUSS

Answer the following questions and discuss your answers when you meet with your team.

1. *Do you agree with the Pareto Principle that your top 20 percent produces 80 percent of your results? Explain.*

_____

_____

_____

2. *How does your organization delegate responsibilities?*

_____

_____

_____

3. *How do you currently prioritize your responsibilities?*

_____

_____

_____

4. *How can you change to be sure you always focus your greatest effort on your top 20 percent?*

_____

_____

_____

APPLY

1. Are you prepared to really shake up your life and get out of your comfort zone in order to live and work according to your priorities? Is there something in your life that is working so poorly that you intuitively know it will require a major revision in how you do things? What is that something? Describe *how* it is not working. Describe *why* it is not working. Can you think outside the box (or create a new box) to solve the issue and realign your priorities? Ignoring a major alignment problem in your priorities is like lining up a golf shot incorrectly. Just as the farther you hit the ball, the more off course it will be, the longer you live out of alignment, the greater the chance you will miss achieving your vision.

2. Successful people live according to the Law of Priorities. Successful leaders help their organization, department, or team live according to the Law of Priorities. As the leader, have you taken responsibility for prioritizing and thinking ahead for your area of responsibility? Have you carved out specific time on a regular basis to revisit priorities for that area? If not, you need to start doing so immediately. As a leader, it's not enough for you to be successful. You need to help your people be successful.

TAKE ACTION

It's easier to balance a schedule that has only a few things on it, but leaders and emerging leaders seldom have just a few things on their calendars. If you kept track of your events and project last year, look back at your calendar. If you didn't keep a detailed calendar, try to list the trips you took, projects you worked on, and daily tasks that made up your year. Answer the following questions by referring to that information.

1. *What is required of me?*

    _____

    _____

    _____

2. *What gives the greatest return?*

    _____

    _____

    _____

3. *What brings the greatest reward?*

    _____

    _____

    _____

4. *What tasks that do not bring a high return can I delegate to someone else?*

    _____

    _____

    _____

5. *What tasks that do not bring a high return can be stopped altogether?*

    _____

    _____

    _____

6. *How can I define my top 20 percent priorities?*

    _____

    _____

    _____

7. *How will I dedicate time, energy, and resources to these top priorities?*

_____

_____

_____

8. *What rewards do I expect from focusing on my top priorities?*

_____

_____

_____

9. *Who will I ask to keep me accountable to my top priorities, and how often will we discuss my priorities?*

_____

_____

_____

18

THE LAW OF SACRIFICE

A Leader Must Give Up to Go Up

Sacrifice is a constant in leadership. It is an ongoing process, not a one-time payment. And when leaders look back at their careers, they recognize that there has always been a cost involved in moving forward. Leaders who want continued success must live by the *Law of Sacrifice*.

Why does an individual step forward to lead other people? For every person the answer is different. A few do it to survive. Some do it to make money. Many desire to build a business or organization. Others do it because they want to change the world. That was the reason for Martin Luther King Jr.

King's leadership ability began to emerge when he was in college. He had always been a good student. In high school, he skipped ninth grade. And when he took a college entrance exam as a junior, his scores were high enough that he decided to skip his senior year and enroll in Morehouse College in Atlanta. At age eighteen, he received his ministerial license. At nineteen, he was ordained and received his bachelor's degree in sociology.

King continued his education at Crozer Seminary in Pennsylvania. While he was there, two significant things happened. He heard a message about the life and teachings of Mahatma Gandhi, which forever marked him and put in motion his serious study of the Indian leader. He also emerged as a leader among his peers and was elected president of the senior class. From there, he studied for his PhD at Boston University. It was also during this time that he married Coretta Scott.

King accepted his first pastorate in Montgomery, Alabama, at the Dexter Avenue Baptist Church in 1954, and settled into family life when his first child was born the next year in November. But that peace didn't last long. Less than a month later, Rosa Parks refused to relinquish her seat on a bus to a white passenger and was arrested. Local African-American leaders arranged a one-day boycott of the transit system to protest her arrest and the city's segregation policy. When it was successful, they decided to create the Montgomery Improvement Association (MIA) to continue the boycott. Already recognized as a leader in the community, King was unanimously elected president of the newly formed organization.

For the next year, King led African-American community leaders in a boycott with the goal of changing the system. The MIA negotiated with city leaders and demanded courteous treatment of African-Americans by bus operators, first-come, first-served seating for all bus riders, and employment of African-American bus drivers. While the boycott was on, community leaders organized carpools, raised funds to support the boycott financially, rallied and mobilized the community with sermons, and coordinated legal challenges with the NAACP. Finally in November 1956, the U.S. Supreme Court struck down the laws allowing segregated seating on buses.[1] King and the other leaders were successful. Their world was beginning to change.

The Montgomery bus boycott was a major step in the American civil rights movement, and it's easy to see what was gained as a result of it. But King also began paying a personal cost for it. Soon after the boycott began, King was arrested for a minor traffic violation. A bomb was thrown onto his porch. And he was indicted on a charge of being party to a conspiracy to hinder and prevent the operation of business without "just or legal cause."[2] King was emerging as a leader, but he was paying a price for it.

Each time King climbed higher and moved forward in leadership for the cause of civil rights, the greater the price he paid for it. His wife, Coretta Scott King, remarked in *My Life with Martin Luther King, Jr.*, "Day and night our phone would ring, and someone would pour out a string of obscene epithets . . . Frequently the calls ended with a threat to kill us if we didn't get out of town. But in spite of all the danger, the chaos of our private lives, I felt inspired, almost elated."

King did some great things as a leader. He met with presidents. He delivered rousing speeches that are considered some of the most outstanding examples of oration in American history. He led 250,000 people in a peaceful march on Washington, D.C. He received the Nobel Peace Prize. And he did create change in this country. But the Law of Sacrifice demands that the greater the leader, the more he must give up. During that same period, King was arrested many times and jailed on many occasions. He was stoned, stabbed, and physically attacked. His house was bombed. Yet his vision—and his influence—continued to increase. Ultimately, he sacrificed everything he had. But what he gave up he parted with willingly. In his last speech, delivered the night before he was assassinated in Memphis, he said,

> I don't know what will happen to me now. We've got some difficult days ahead. But it doesn't matter to me now. Because I've been to the mountaintop. I won't mind. Like anybody else, I would like to live a long life. Longevity has its place. But I'm not concerned about that now. I just want to do God's will. And He's allowed me to go up to the mountain. And I've looked over and I've seen the Promised Land. I may not get there with you, but I want you to know tonight that we, as a people, will get to the Promised Land. So I'm happy tonight . . . I'm not fearing any man. "Mine eyes have seen the glory of the coming of the Lord."[3]

The next day he paid the ultimate price of sacrifice.

King's impact was profound. He influenced millions of people to peacefully stand up against a system and society that fought to exclude them. The United States has changed for the better because of his leadership.

OBSERVE

You have to give up to go up. The true nature of leadership is really sacrifice.

1. *What were some of the sacrifices King made?*

_____

_____

_____

2. *How did King's level of sacrifice increase as his influence increased?*

_____

_____

_____

3. *How did King's sacrifice impact those who followed him? Those who opposed him?*

_____

_____

_____

4. *What sacrifices have leaders in your profession or area of service made? Have these sacrifices paid off?*

_____

_____

_____

LEARN

There is a common misperception among people who aren't leaders that leadership is all about the position, perks, and power that come from rising in an organization. Many people today want to climb up the corporate ladder because they believe that freedom, power, and wealth are the prizes waiting at the top. The life of a leader can look glamorous to people on the outside. But the reality is that leadership requires sacrifice. A leader must give up to go up. In recent years, we've observed more than our share of leaders who used and abused their organizations for their personal benefit—and the resulting corporate scandals that came because of their greed and selfishness. The heart of good leadership is sacrifice.

If you desire to become the best leader you can be, then you need to be willing to make sacrifices in order to lead well. If that is your desire, then here are some things you need to know about the Law of Sacrifice:

1. THERE IS NO SUCCESS WITHOUT SACRIFICE

Every person who has achieved any success in life has made sacrifices to do so. Many working people dedicate four or more years and pay thousands of dollars to attend college to get the tools they'll need before embarking on their career. Athletes sacrifice countless hours in the gym and on the practice field preparing themselves to perform at a high level. Parents give up much of their free time and sacrifice their resources in order to do a good job raising their children. Philosopher-poet Ralph Waldo Emerson observed, "For everything you have missed, you have gained something else; and for everything you gain, you lose something." Life is a series of trades, one thing for another.

Leaders must give up to go up. That's true of every leader regardless of profession. Talk to leaders, and you will find that they have made repeated sacrifices. Effective leaders sacrifice much that is good in order to dedicate themselves to what is best. That's the way the Law of Sacrifice works.

2. LEADERS ARE OFTEN ASKED TO GIVE UP MORE THAN OTHERS

The heart of leadership is putting others ahead of yourself. It's doing what is best for the team. For that reason, I believe that leaders have to give up their rights. As Gerald Brooks, leadership speaker and pastor, says, "When you become a leader, you lose the right to think about yourself." Visually, it looks like this.

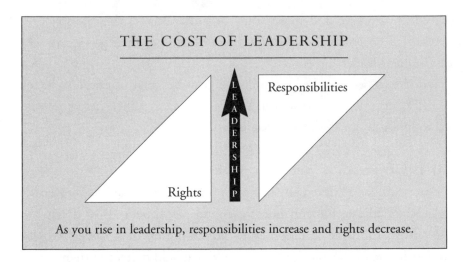

THE COST OF LEADERSHIP

Responsibilities

L
E
A
D
E
R
S
H
I
P

Rights

As you rise in leadership, responsibilities increase and rights decrease.

When you have no responsibilities, you can do pretty much anything you want. Once you take on responsibility, you start to experience limitations in what you can do. The more responsibility you accept, the fewer options you have.

Digital Chairman and Chief Executive Robert Palmer said in an interview, "In my model of management, there's very little wiggle room. If you want a management job, then you have to accept the responsibility and accountability that goes with it."[4] He is really talking about the cost of leadership. Leaders must be willing to give up more than the people they lead.

For every person, the nature of the sacrifice may be different. Everyone who leads gives up other opportunities. Some people have to give up beloved hobbies. Many give up aspects of their personal lives. Some, like King, give their actual lives. The circumstances are different from person to person, but the principle doesn't change. Leadership means sacrifice.

3. YOU MUST KEEP GIVING UP TO STAY UP

Most people are willing to acknowledge that sacrifices are necessary early in a leadership career in order to make progress. They'll take an undesirable territory to make a name for themselves. They'll move their family to a less desirable city to accept a better position. They'll take a temporary cut in pay for greater opportunities for advancement. The problem for leaders comes when they think they have earned the right to stop making sacrifices. But in leadership, sacrifice is an ongoing process, not a one-time payment.

If leaders have to give up to go up, then they have to give up even more to stay up. Have you ever considered how infrequently sports teams have back-to-back championship seasons? The reason is simple: if a leader can win one championship with his team, he often assumes he can duplicate the results the next year by doing the same things. He becomes reluctant to make additional sacrifices in the off-season to prepare for what is often an even greater challenge the next year. But today's success is the greatest threat to tomorrow's success. And what gets a team to the top isn't what keeps it there. The only way to stay up is to give up even more. Leadership success requires continual change, constant improvement, and ongoing sacrifice.

4. The Higher the Level of Leadership, the Greater the Sacrifice
Have you ever been part of an auction? It's an exciting experience. An item comes up for a bid, and everyone in the room gets excited. When the bidding opens, lots of people jump in and take part. But as the price goes higher and higher, what happens? There are fewer and fewer bidders. When the price is low, everybody bids. In the end, only one person is willing to pay the high price that the item actually costs. It's the same in leadership: the higher you go, the more it's going to cost you. And it doesn't matter what kind of leadership career you pick. You will have to make sacrifices. You will have to give up to go up.

There can be no success without sacrifice. Anytime you see success, you can be sure someone made sacrifices to make it possible. And as a leader, if you sacrifice, even if you don't witness the success, you can be sure that someone in the future will benefit from what you've given.

DISCUSS

Answer the following questions and discuss your answers when you meet with your team.

1. *What is the premise for the Law of Sacrifice?*

   _____

   _____

   _____

2. *Do you agree that in order to move forward you will have to give something up? Explain.*

   _____

   _____

   _____

3. *Why do your rights decrease as your responsibilities increase?*

   _____

   _____

   _____

4. *Give an example of something you had to give up in order to reach a goal you set for yourself.*

   _____

   _____

   _____

5. *What have successful leaders in your organization given up in order to move forward or maintain their leadership?*

   _____

   _____

   _____

6. *What one thing could you give up today that would move you closer to a goal you have set for yourself? Explain how you will commit to sacrificing this thing.*

_____

_____

_____

APPLY

1. To become a more influential leader, are you willing to make sacrifices? Are you willing to give up your rights for the sake of the people you lead? Give it some thought. Then create two lists: (1) the things you are willing to give up in order to go up, and (2) the things you are *not* willing to sacrifice to advance. Be sure to consider which list will contain items such as your health, marriage, relationships with children, finances, and so on.

2. Living by the Law of Sacrifice usually means being willing to trade something of value that you possess to gain something more valuable that you don't. King gave up many personal freedoms to gain freedoms for others. In order to make such sacrificial trades, an individual must have something of value to trade. What do you have to offer? And what are you currently willing to trade your time, energy, and resources to get that may give you greater personal worth?

3. One of the most harmful mind-sets of leaders is what I call destination disease—the idea that they can sacrifice for a season and then "arrive." Leaders who think this way stop sacrificing and stop gaining higher ground in leadership.

In what areas might you be in danger of having destination disease? Write them down. Then for each, create a statement of ongoing growth that will be an antidote to such thinking. For example, if you have the mind-set that you finish learning once you graduate from school, you may need to write, "I will make it my practice to learn and grow in one significant area every year."

TAKE ACTION

The Law of Sacrifice can be seen in almost any diet or financial plan. You stop eating certain things to lose weight. You don't go to the movies every weekend so you can take the family on vacation in the summer. And just like food and money, time is also a commodity. Earl Nightingale says that if a person studied one hour a day for three years on a single topic, that he or she would become an expert in that field. But what would that person have to give up in order to spend the time studying?

This week, you are to find one thing in your life that if you gave it up you believe it will move you forward. This is not limited to leadership. Moving forward might mean giving up your weekend golf game to spend more time with your family—investing in relationships. You could commit to waking up an hour earlier every morning to exercise—investing in your health. Or you could carve out one hour each day to learn about something that would advance your leadership and value to others—investing in your personal growth.

Fill in the blanks and commit to being committed!

For 6 months I will give up

_____

and instead I will

_____

My goal is to

_____

_____

I will tell _____ *about my progress, and ask this person to keep me accountable.*

19

THE LAW OF TIMING

*When to Lead Is As Important As
What to Do and Where to Go*

W HEN THE STAKES ARE HIGH, THE CONSEQUENCES OF THE LAW OF TIMING are dramatic and immediate. Reading a situation and knowing what to do are not enough to make you succeed in leadership. If you want your organization, department, or team to move forward, you must pay attention to timing. Only the right action *at the right time* will bring success. Anything else exacts a high price.

READ

If ever there was an example of the importance of timing as it relates to leadership, it came in New Orleans in late August and early September of 2005.

New Orleans is an unusual city. Like Venice, Italy, it is surrounded by water. To the north lies Lake Pontchartrain. To the south flows the mighty Mississippi River. To the east and west are low-lying swamplands. Canals crisscross the city. You cannot drive into or out of New Orleans with crossing a major bridge. That may not seem like a big deal—until you consider that most of the city lies below sea level. New Orleans is shaped like a bowl. On average, the city is six feet below sea level. In the lowest areas, it's nine feet below sea level. And the land in New Orleans sinks a little more every year. For decades citizens have worried about the potential damage that a direct hit from a powerful hurricane could do to the city.

On Wednesday, August 24, 2005, nobody in New Orleans could have known that the newly formed tropical storm, named Katrina, would be the big one—the hurricane the city had feared would someday come. It wasn't until Friday that the National Hurricane Center predicted that the storm would reach landfall on Monday somewhere near Buras, Louisiana, about sixty miles southeast of New Orleans. The hurricane was already looking like a bad one. The next morning, Saturday, August 27, the leaders of many of Louisiana's parishes around New Orleans ordered mandatory evacuations: St. Charles, Plaquemines, parts of Jefferson, and even St. Tammany, which is situated on higher ground north of New Orleans.

But what about New Orleans? Why didn't Mayor Ray Nagin, the leader of the city, order a mandatory evacuation at the same time? Many people say New Orleanians are fatalistic and they can't be made to move any faster than they want to go. Others say that Nagin, a businessman before he was elected, was worried about the legal and financial implications of an evacuation. I say he and others in government didn't understand the Law of Timing. When to lead is as important as what to do and where to go.

The time to move people out of New Orleans was when the other parish leaders announced their mandatory evacuations. Nagin waited. On Saturday evening, he finally announced a *voluntary* evacuation of New Orleans. Only after Max Mayfield, the director of the National Hurricane Center, called Nagin on Saturday night did the mayor become concerned enough to act. "Max scared the crap out of me," Nagin is reported to have said after the call.[1]

The next morning at nine o'clock, Nagin finally ordered a mandatory evacuation—fewer than twenty-four hours before the hurricane would make landfall. It was much too late for many citizens of New Orleans. And how did he plan to help those people who couldn't make it out of town on such short notice? He advised them to get to the Superdome, the city's shelter of last resort, however they could. But he made no real provisions for them. In a press conference Nagin advised,

> If you can't leave the city and you have to come to the Superdome, come with enough food, [non]perishable items to last for three to five days. Come with blankets, with pillows. No weapons, no alcohol, no drugs. You know, this is like the governor said, you're going on a camping trip. If you don't know what that's like,

just bring enough stuff for you to be able to sleep and be comfortable. It's not going to be the best environment, but at least you will be safe.[2]

The results of Nagin's leadership played out in the national coverage of Katrina and its aftermath. Water was flowing into parts of the city by 9:00 a.m. Monday morning. Conditions for the people at the Superdome were dreadful. Other people who couldn't get out of town flocked to the Convention Center. Many citizens were stranded on rooftops. How did Nagin respond? He complained to the media at press conferences.

If someone was going to step in and lead, it would have to occur somewhere other than the local level. Most people began looking to the federal government for leadership, but they violated the Law of Timing too. Not until Wednesday, August 31, did Director of Homeland Security Michael Chertoff release a memo declaring Katrina an "Incident of National Significance"—a key designation needed to trigger swift federal coordination.[3] President Bush didn't meet with his cabinet until the following day to determine how to launch the White House Task Force on Hurricane Katrina Response. Meanwhile, the people stranded in New Orleans waited for help. On Thursday, September 1, the Red Cross requested permission to take water, food, and supplies to the people who were stranded in the city, but their request was denied by the Louisiana office of Homeland Security. They were asked to wait another day.[4] Finally, on Sunday, September 4—six days after New Orleans flooded—the evacuation of the Superdome was finally complete.

The way Katrina was handled shows leadership timing at its worst. It was botched at every level. Even the local animal shelter did better than the mayor. Two days prior to Katrina's arrival, it evacuated hundreds of animals to Houston, Texas.[5] In the end, more than 1,836 people died as a result of the hurricane; 1,577 of those people were from Louisiana.[6] Eighty percent of the deaths in Louisiana occurred in Orleans and St. Bernard parishes, with the overwhelming majority occurring in New Orleans.[7] If the leaders had paid greater attention not only to *what* they did but also to *when* they did it, many more lives would have been saved.

OBSERVE

Reading a situation and knowing what to do are not enough to make you succeed in leadership. Only the right action at the right time will bring success.

1. *How did Nagin's hesitation impact the people he led?*

   _____

   _____

   _____

2. *How did the federal government violate the Law of Timing in their response to Katrina?*

   _____

   _____

   _____

3. *Do you agree with the author's statement "If the leaders had paid greater attention not only to what they did but also to when they did it, many more lives would have been saved"? Explain.*

   _____

   _____

   _____

4. *Give an example of how the Law of Timing has worked against someone in your profession or area of service.*

   _____

   _____

   _____

5. *What is happening in your profession or industry now that will require attention to timing?*

_____

_____

_____

LEARN

Good leaders recognize that *when* to lead is as important as what to do and where to go. Timing is often the difference between success and failure in an endeavor.

Every time a leader makes a move, there are really only four outcomes:

1. THE WRONG ACTION AT THE WRONG TIME LEADS TO DISASTER

A leader who takes the wrong action at the wrong time is sure to suffer negative repercussions. That was certainly the case in New Orleans as Katrina approached. Nagin's poor leadership set in motion a series of wrong actions at the wrong time. He waited until it was too late to call for a mandatory evacuation. He sent faxes to local churches, hoping they would help with evacuating people, but by the time he did so, the people who would have received the faxes were already long gone. He picked a poor location for the shelter of last resort, neglected to supply it properly, and failed to provide adequate transportation for people to get there. One wrong action after another led to disaster.

Obviously, the stakes for every leadership decision are not as high as they were for Mayor Nagin. But every leadership situation requires that leaders heed the Law of Timing. If you lead a department or a small team and you take the wrong action at the wrong time, your people will suffer. And so will your leadership.

2. THE RIGHT ACTION AT THE WRONG TIME BRINGS RESISTANCE

When it comes to good leadership, having a vision for the direction of the organization or team and knowing how to get there aren't enough. If you take the right action but do it at the wrong time, you may still be unsuccessful because the people you lead can become resistant.

Good leadership timing requires many things:

- Understanding—leaders must have a firm grasp on the situation.
- Maturity—if leaders' motives aren't right, their timing will be off.
- Confidence—people follow leaders who *know* what must be done.
- Decisiveness—wishy-washy leaders create wishy-washy followers.
- Experience—if leaders don't possess experience, then they need to gain wisdom from others who do possess it.
- Intuition—timing often depends on intangibles, such as momentum and morale.
- Preparation—if the conditions aren't right, leaders must create those conditions.

3. The Wrong Action at the Right Time Is a Mistake

People who are naturally entrepreneurial often possess a strong sense of timing. They intuitively know when it's time to make a move—to seize an opportunity. They sometimes make mistakes in their actions at those key moments. My brother, Larry, who is an excellent businessman, has coached me in this area. Larry says that the greatest mistake made by entrepreneurs and other people in business is knowing when to cut their losses or when to increase their investment to maximize their gains. Their mistakes come from taking the wrong action at the right time.

Once again, I have experience in this area. Because I'm known primarily as a communicator, for years people tried to talk me into doing a radio program. For a long time I resisted the idea. In the mid-1990s, however, I could see there was a need for a growth-oriented program for people of faith. So we decided to create a program called *Growing Today*. The problem was the format. Most programs of that type are supported by donations, but I believe in free-market economics. I wanted the program to support itself by selling products, the way any other commercial program would. What a mistake. The show never broke even. It was the right time, but the wrong idea. The Law of Timing had spoken again.

4. The Right Action at the Right Time Results in Success

When the right leader and the right timing come together, incredible things happen. An organization achieves its goals, reaps incredible rewards, and gains momentum.

Success almost becomes inevitable. If you look at the history of nearly any organization, you will find a pivotal moment when the right leader took the right action at the right time, and it transformed the organization. Winston Churchill, whose greatness in leadership depended on the Law of Timing, described the impact that leaders can make—and the satisfaction they can experience—when they take the right action at the right time. He said, "There comes a special moment in everyone's life, a moment for which that person was born. That special opportunity, when he seizes it, will fulfill his mission—a mission for which he is uniquely qualified. In that moment, he finds greatness. It is his finest hour." Every leader desires to experience that moment.

DISCUSS

Answer the following questions and discuss your answers when you meet with your team.

1. *What happens if you have the right idea, but you try to implement it at the wrong time?*

2. *What happens if you know it's time to do something, but choose the wrong thing to do? Give an example from your profession or area of service.*

3. *Do you agree with the author that timing is just as important as what you do? Explain.*

4. *Up until now, how did you take timing into account when making a decision?*

_____

_____

_____

5. *How do you think examining the timing of a decision will affect your leadership in the future?*

_____

_____

_____

6. *What will you do to make sure that to the best of your ability your timing is right?*

_____

_____

_____

APPLY

1. It has been said that managers do things right while leaders do the right things. The Law of Timing says that leaders do more than that: they do the right things at the right time. In your approach to leadership, does timing play an important part in your strategy? Do you think about the appropriateness of the timing as much as you do the rightness of the action? Review the major actions you've initiated in the recent past, and discern how much attention you've given to timing.

2. Spend some time analyzing recent failed initiatives for your organization, department, or team to determine whether they were caused by the wrong action or the wrong timing. (These initiatives can be yours or others'.) To help you, answer the following questions:

What was the goal of the initiative?
Who was the individual responsible for leading it?

What factors were taken into account while the strategy was planned?

Whose experience did the strategy draw upon?

What was the condition or temperature of the organization at the time of the launch?

What were the market or industry conditions?

What "leverage" was available and being used to aid in the initiative?

What factors were clearly working against it?

Might the initiative have been more successful had it been launched either earlier or later?

Why did the initiative ultimately fail?

3. AS YOU PREPARE TO ENGAGE IN FUTURE PLANS, USE THE LIST OF FACTORS FROM THE CHAPTER TO PREPARE FOR THE TIMING OF YOUR ACTIONS:

- Understanding: Do you have a firm grasp on the situation?
- Maturity: Are your motives right?
- Confidence: Do you believe in what you are doing?
- Decisiveness: Can you initiate action with confidence and win people's trust?
- Experience: Have you drawn upon wisdom from others to inform your strategy?
- Intuition: Have you taken into account intangibles such as momentum and morale?
- Preparation: Have you done everything you must to set up your team for success?

Remember, only the right action at the right time will bring success to your team, department, or organization.

TAKE ACTION

Some of the most intriguing motives contain plots that are enhanced by using the Law of Timing. Murder mysteries, westerns, and action adventure movies all rely on certain characters learning about what another character has done at a certain time, having the primary characters at a certain place at a certain time, and watching the hero take just the right steps at the right time in order to succeed.

This week, watch one of your favorite action movies. Take notes on how the Law of Timing played a role in success and failure.

Law of Timing moment:

_____

_____

_____

What would have happened if the character had timed things differently?

_____

_____

_____

20

THE LAW OF EXPLOSIVE GROWTH

To Add Growth, Lead Followers—To Multiply, Lead Leaders

I HAVEN'T ALWAYS FELT THE WAY I DO NOW ABOUT LEADERSHIP. MY BELIEF in the power of leadership and my passion for training leaders have been developed over the course of my professional life. When I started in my career, I thought personal growth was the key to being able to make an impact. My father had been very strategic in my development as I was growing up. He actually paid me to read books that he knew would help me and sent me to conferences when I was a teenager. Those experiences provided a great foundation for me. And after I began working, I discovered the Law of Process. That prompted me to take a pro-active approach to my personal growth.

As a result, when people asked me to help them be more successful, I focused on teaching personal growth. It wasn't until I was forty years old that I began to understand the Law of the Inner Circle and the importance of developing a team. That's when my ability to grow an organization and reach greater goals began to increase. But it wasn't until I began to focus on developing leaders that my leadership really took off. I had discovered the Law of Explosive Growth: to add growth, lead followers—to multiply, lead leaders.

READ

In 1990, I traveled to a country in South America with my wife, Margaret, to teach leadership in a national conference. One of the great joys of my life is teaching leadership to people of influence who desire to make a difference. I was really looking forward to this conference because it was an opportunity to add value to people outside my regular sphere of influence. But it didn't turn out the way I expected.

Everything started well. The people were very gracious, and I was able to connect with them despite the language and cultural barriers. But it wasn't long before I could tell that the attendees and I were not on the same page. When I started to teach about leadership, I could tell my comments were not connecting with them. They didn't engage, and what I was trying to communicate didn't seem to make an impact.

My read on the situation was confirmed after my first session with them. As I spoke with individuals, they didn't want to talk about leadership issues. They didn't ask questions about growing their organizations or fulfilling a vision. They sought advice about personal issues, problems, and conflicts with other people. I felt that I was back doing personal counseling similar to what I did at the beginning of my career. For the next three days, I grew more and more frustrated. The people I spoke to didn't understand leadership, and they had no desire to learn anything about it. For someone like me who believes that everything rises and falls on leadership, it drove me crazy!

This wasn't the first time I had experienced such frustration. I noticed that whenever I traveled to developing countries, I faced similar situations. I suspect that in nations where there is no strong business infrastructure and where government doesn't allow the citizens much freedom, it is difficult for leaders to develop.

On the flight home, I talked to Margaret about all my frustrations. I finally summed it up, saying, "I don't want to do this anymore. I traveled thousands of miles just to counsel people on petty conflicts. If they would just turn their attention to becoming leaders, it would change their lives."

After listening patiently, Margaret replied, "Maybe you're the one who's supposed to do something about this."

Margaret's exhortation to do something about the leadership problems I had seen overseas stirred something within me. For the next several years, I reflected on the issue and thought about possible solutions. Finally in 1996, I decided what I would do. I brought together a group of leaders to help me create a not-for-profit organization to develop leaders in government, education, and the religious community. I named it EQUIP—encouraging qualities undeveloped in people.

For the next five years, EQUIP made modest progress in its goals. But in the months after the terrorist attacks of September 11, 2001, we went through a difficult period in which we had to lay off half the staff. But we took that as an opportunity to reexamine our priorities. We narrowed our focus and developed a new goal—one so large and daunting it looked almost impossible. We would try to develop *one million leaders* around the globe by 2008. How could a small nonprofit organization hope to accomplish such a feat? By using the Law of Explosive Growth!

EQUIP's strategy, which came to be called the Million Leader Mandate, was to develop 40,000 leaders in countries around the world. Those leaders would attend a training session every six months in a city near them for three years. The only thing that would be asked of them in return was that they commit to personally develop twenty-five leaders in their own city, town, or village. EQUIP would provide the training materials for the 40,000 leaders it trained, *and* it would provide materials for the twenty-five leaders each of them would be developing.

EQUIP already employed some excellent leaders, including John Hull, president and CEO; Doug Carter, senior vice president; and Tim Elmore, vice president of leadership development. They assembled a top-notch team and began creating the training materials. Then they formed strategic alliances with organizations overseas. These organizations would help EQUIP figure out the cities in which to do the training, identify country and city coordinators to run the training sessions, and identify and recruit the 40,000 leaders to be trained.

The final step was to recruit excellent leaders who would be willing to volunteer their time to do the training in these cities around the world. Two trainers would travel to a city twice a year for three years, paying their own way and donating funds to help underwrite the materials the attendees would need. They would train the 40,000 who would in turn train twenty-five each. If the strategy succeeded, we would develop one million leaders. It was an ambitious plan. The question was, would it work?

Convinced that developing leaders was the key to reaching our goal of training a million leaders, EQUIP launched the MLM initiative in 2002 in several cities in India, Indonesia, and the Philippines. We had chosen those areas because we had the best contacts there and had experienced success there in previous years. The response was overwhelming. Hundreds of hungry leaders traveled to each site to engage in the two-day training. Some attendees spent as many as five days *walking* to get to the event! And at the end of the training when we asked attendees to commit to developing twenty-five leaders over the next three years using the materials we would give them, more than 90 percent of the attendees signed on.

With the first success under our belt, we moved forward. The next year we began training leaders in other parts of Asia and the Middle East. In 2004, we started training in Africa; in 2005, Europe; and in 2006, South America. On every continent, the strategy was the same:

1. Connect with key influential leaders in organizations already working with people locally and enlist their assistance.
2. Ask those key leaders to identify the cities in their country in which to do the training and to host the training events.
3. Rely on those key leaders to recruit leaders to attend the training.
4. Recruit leaders in the U.S. willing to travel overseas to train leaders and support the effort financially.
5. Receive a commitment from local attendees to find and train leaders for three years while we trained them.

In some cities, we had very modest success, with a few dozen leaders attending the training. In other cities, people came by the hundreds. Many leaders were able to commit to developing twenty-five leaders. Some could commit to training only five or ten. But others were training 100, 200, or 250 in their towns and cities!

As I mentioned, we wanted to reach our goal of training one million leaders by 2008. At times, it was a struggle. In some countries we had a difficult time gaining credibility. In others it took us a long time to make connections with leaders. But to our great surprise and delight, in the spring of 2006 we reached our goal—two years ahead of schedule! Now what seemed to be an impossible goal seems modest. In 2007, we trained our second million. And we launched an initiative to develop 5 million leaders in five years. My hope and prayer are that before I'm finished, EQUIP and its partners will train 50 million leaders around the globe. *That's* explosive growth.

OBSERVE

No matter where you are, I know one thing: You will be able to reach your potential and help your organization reach its loftiest goals only if you begin developing leaders instead of merely attracting followers. Leaders who develop leaders experience an incredible multiplication effect in their organizations that can be achieved in no other way—not by increasing resources, reducing costs, increasing profit margins, improving systems, implementing quality procedures, or doing anything else. The only way to experience an explosive level of growth is to do the math—leader's math.

1. *Why is leadership the key to growth?*

_____

_____

_____

2. *Why has the Million Leader Mandate been successful?*

_____

_____

_____

3. *What organization in your field has experienced explosive growth and sustained growth? How did they grow so quickly?*

_____

_____

_____

4. *What is the current focus in your organization: leading leaders or followers?*

_____

_____

_____

LEARN

Leaders are naturally impatient. At least, all of the leaders I know are. Leaders want to move fast. They want to see the vision fulfilled. They delight in progress. Good leaders quickly assess where an organization is, project where it needs to go, and have strong ideas about how to get it there. The problem is that most of the time the people and the organization lag behind the leader. For that reason, leaders always feel a tension between where they and their people *are* and where they *ought to be.* I have experienced this tension my entire life. In every organization I've ever been a part of, I had a strong sense of where it should go. I even felt that way as a kid. (I wasn't always *right* about where we should go, but I always thought I *knew!*)

How do you relieve that tension between where the organization is and where you want it to be? The answer can be found in the Law of Explosive Growth:

If you develop yourself, you can experience personal success.
If you develop a team, your organization can experience growth.
If you develop leaders, your organization can achieve explosive growth.

You can grow by leading followers. But if you want to maximize your leadership and help your organization reach its potential, you need to develop leaders. There is no other way to experience explosive growth.

A DIFFERENT FOCUS

Becoming a leader who develops leaders requires an entirely different focus and attitude from simply attracting and leading followers. It takes a different mind-set. Consider some of the differences between leaders who attract followers and leaders who develop leaders:

Leaders Who Attract Followers . . . Need to Be Needed
Leaders Who Develop Leaders . . . Want to Be Succeeded
Excitement comes from becoming a leader. When you speak, people listen. When you want to get something done, you can enlist other people to help you. Having followers can make you feel needed and important. However, that is a pretty shallow reason to pursue leadership. Good leaders lead for the sake of their followers and for what they can leave behind after their time of leadership is completed.

Leaders Who Attract Followers . . . Develop the Bottom 20 Percent
Leaders Who Develop Leaders . . . Develop the Top 20 Percent
When you're leading a group of people, who typically asks for the most time and attention? The weakest ones in the group. If you allow them to, they will consume 80 percent or more of your time. However, proactive leaders who practice the Law of Explosive Growth don't allow that bottom 20 percent to take all their time. They seek out the *best* 20 percent—the people with the greatest leadership potential—and they invest their time developing them. They know that if they develop the best, the best will help with the rest.

Leaders Who Attract Followers . . . Focus on Weaknesses
Leaders Who Develop Leaders . . . Focus on Strengths
A necessity of working with the bottom 20 percent is that you must continually deal with their weaknesses. Unsuccessful people usually need help with the basics. Problems in those areas keep them from achieving consistent performance on a regular basis. However, when you work with your best people, you can build on their strengths.

Leaders Who Attract Followers . . . Treat Everyone the Same
Leaders Who Develop Leaders . . . Treat Individuals Differently
There is a myth in some leadership circles that promotes the idea of treating everyone the same for the sake of "fairness." What a mistake. As Mick Delaney says, "Any business or industry that pays equal rewards to its goof-offs and its eager beavers sooner or later will find itself with more goof-offs than eager beavers." Leaders who develop leaders give rewards, resources, and responsibility based on results. The greater the impact of leaders, the greater the opportunities they receive.

Leaders Who Attract Followers . . . Spend Time with Others

Leaders Who Develop Leaders . . . Invest Time in Others

Leaders who attract only followers and never develop them don't increase the value of those they lead. However, when leaders take time to develop the leaders they attract, they are making a valuable investment in them. Every moment they spend helps to increase their ability and influence. And that pays dividends to them and the organization.

Leaders Who Attract Followers . . . Grow by Addition

Leaders Who Develop Leaders . . . Grow by Multiplication

Leaders who attract followers grow their organization only one person at a time. When you attract one follower, you impact one person. And you receive the value and power of one person. However, leaders who develop leaders multiply their organization's growth, because for every leader they develop, they also receive the value of all of that leader's followers.

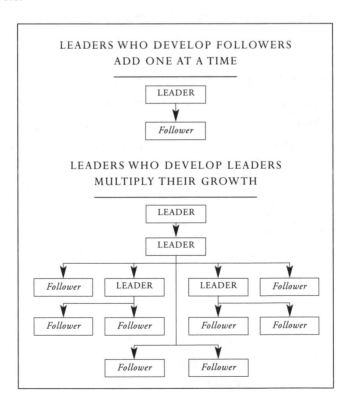

Add ten followers to your organization, and you have the power of ten people. Add ten leaders to your organization, and you have the power of ten leaders times all of the followers and leaders *they* influence. That's what I call leader's math. It's the difference between addition and multiplication. It's like growing your organization by teams instead of by individuals.

Leaders Who Attract Followers . . . Impact Only People They Touch
Leaders Who Develop Leaders . . . Impact People Beyond Their Reach
Leaders who attract followers but never develop leaders get tired. Why? Because they themselves must deal with every person under their authority. Being able to impact only the people you can touch personally is very limiting. In contrast, leaders who develop leaders impact people far beyond their personal reach. The better the leaders they develop, the greater the quality and quantity of followers and the greater the reach. Every time you develop leaders and help them increase their leadership ability, you make them capable of influencing an even greater number of people. By helping one person, you can reach many others.

THE CHALLENGE OF LEADING LEADERS

If developing leaders has such a great impact, then why doesn't everyone do it? Because it's hard! Leadership development isn't an add water and stir proposition. It takes a lot of time, energy, and resources. Here's why:

1. LEADERS ARE HARD TO FIND

How many people do you know who are really good leaders? They have influence. They make things happen. They see and seize opportunities. And they can attract, enlist, and rally people to perform with excellence. There just aren't that many people capable of doing that on a consistent basis. Most people are followers. Some are producers. Few are leaders. Leaders are like eagles—they don't flock. That's why they are so hard to find.

2. LEADERS ARE HARD TO GATHER

Once you find leaders, drawing them in can be very difficult. They are entrepreneurial and want to go their own way. If you try to recruit them, they want to know where you're going, how you plan to get there, who else you're planning to take with you—and whether they can drive! What you're doing has to be more compelling than what they're already doing.

On top of that, your organization needs to create an environment that is attractive to them. That is often not the case. Most organizations desire stability. Leaders want excitement. Most organizations desire structure. Leaders want flexibility. Most organizations place a high value on following rules. Leaders want to think outside the box. If you want to gather leaders, you must create a place where they can thrive.

3. LEADERS ARE HARD TO KEEP

As hard as it is to find and gather good leaders, it's even more difficult to keep them. The only way to lead leaders is to become a better leader yourself. If you keep growing and stay ahead of the people you lead, then you will be able to keep adding value to the leaders who follow you. Your goal must be to keep developing them so that they can realize their potential. Only a leader can do that for another leader, because it takes a leader to raise up another leader.

One year in my leadership conferences, I took an informal poll to find out what prompted the attendees to become leaders. The results were as follows:

Natural gifting	10 percent
Result of crisis	5 percent
Influence of another leader	85 percent

Only one leader in ten is able to blossom without the help of another leader. The rest need the help of other leaders who are ahead of them in the journey. If you keep adding value to the leaders you lead, then they will be willing to stay with you. Do that long enough, and they may never want to leave.

DISCUSS

Answer the following questions and discuss your answers when you meet with your team.

1. *What is leader's math?*

   _____

   _____

   _____

2. *Why do some leaders prefer to lead followers instead of leading leaders?*

   _____

   _____

   _____

3. *Do you agree with the author's description of leaders who develop followers and leaders who develop leaders? Explain.*

   _____

   _____

   _____

4. *Why would "being fair" not always be the right choice for a leader?*

   _____

   _____

   _____

5. *How has your organization's leadership contributed to the growth and progress of the company?*

   _____

   _____

   _____

6. *How do you feel about being succeeded?*

_____

_____

_____

7. *What attitude or views about leadership do you need to adjust in order to lead leaders?*

_____

_____

_____

APPLY

1. In which stage of the leadership development process do you currently find yourself?

Stage 1: Developing yourself
Stage 2: Developing your team
Stage 3: Developing leaders

To validate your answer, cite specific actions you have taken to develop yourself; to develop a team; and to help specific individuals improve their leadership ability. If you haven't begun to develop leaders, try to identify reasons why. Are you someone who needs to be needed, focuses on the bottom 20 percent, tries to treat everyone the same, or isn't strategic about investing in others? If you aren't developing leaders, identify what steps you must take to get started.

2. What are you currently doing to find and gather leaders? Are there places you go, events you attend, and networks you plug into to look for potential leaders? If not, start looking for some. If so, then what do you do to connect with leaders and recruit them for your organization, department, or team?

3. What are you doing to gather and hold leaders? Are you becoming a better

leader so that leaders will want to follow you? Are you trying to create an environment where leaders can thrive and succeed? Are you giving leaders freedom to lead and be innovative? Are you clearing away red tape? Are you providing them with resources and greater responsibilities? Are you praising risk and rewarding success?

TAKE ACTION

One of the keys to leading leaders is being able to identify a person's leadership potential. Dale Carnegie, a master at identifying potential leaders, once said, "Men are developed the same way gold is mined. Several tons of dirt must be moved to get an ounce of gold. But you don't go in to the mine looking for dirt. You go in looking for the gold."

This week use the following assessment to evaluate and identify the potential leaders on your team. These are the people you want to spend time investing in and developing to become future leaders for your organization.

0 = Never   1= Seldom   2 = Sometimes   3 = Usually   4 = Always

1. The person has influence.	0 1 2 3 4
2. The person has self-discipline.	0 1 2 3 4
3. The person has a good track record.	0 1 2 3 4
4. The person has strong people skills.	0 1 2 3 4
5. The person does not accept the status quo.	0 1 2 3 4
6. The person has the ability to solve problems.	0 1 2 3 4
7. The person sees the big picture.	0 1 2 3 4
8. The person has the ability to handle stress.	0 1 2 3 4
9. The person displays a positive spirit.	0 1 2 3 4
10. The person understands people.	0 1 2 3 4
11. The person is free of personal problems.	0 1 2 3 4
12. The person is willing to take responsibility.	0 1 2 3 4
13. The person is free from anger.	0 1 2 3 4
14. The person is willing to make changes.	0 1 2 3 4

15. The person has integrity.   0 1 2 3 4
16. The person has a strong sense of self.   0 1 2 3 4
17. The person has the ability to see what has to be done next.   0 1 2 3 4
18. The person is accepted as a leader by others.   0 1 2 3 4
19. The person has the ability and desire to keep learning.   0 1 2 3 4
20. The person has a manner that draws people.   0 1 2 3 4
21. The person has a good self-image.   0 1 2 3 4
22. The person has a willingness to serve others.   0 1 2 3 4
23. The person has the ability to develop other leaders.   0 1 2 3 4
24. The person has the ability to bounce back when problems arise. 0 1 2 3 4
25. The person takes initiative.   0 1 2 3 4

TOTAL POINTS _____

When assessing a potential leader, pay more attention to the quality of the person as addressed by the characteristics than to the specific score. Since leaders grade differently, scores vary. This is a general grading scale:

90–100   Great leader
80–89   Good leader
70–79   Emerging leader
60–69   Bursting with potential
Below 60 Needs growth but may not be ready to be mentored as a leader

Direct the 90–100 range people and ask them to mentor the 70–79 range people. Mentor the 80–89 range people yourself. Develop a leadership culture for the rest.

THE LAW OF LEGACY

A Leader's Lasting Value Is Measured by Succession

WHAT DO YOU WANT PEOPLE TO SAY AT YOUR FUNERAL? THAT MAY SEEM like an odd question. But it may be the most important thing you can ask yourself as a leader. Most people never consider it. And that's not good, because if they don't, their lives and leadership can take a direction different from that of their greatest potential and impact. If you want your leadership to really have meaning, you need to take into account the Law of Legacy. Why? Because a leader's lasting value is measured by succession.

READ

In the fall of 1997 on a trip to India with some colleagues, we decided to visit the headquarters of a great leader of the twentieth century: Mother Teresa. Her headquarters, which the local people call the Mother House, is a plain concrete block building located in Kolkata. As I stood outside the doors, I thought that no one could tell by looking at it that this modest place had been the home base of such an effective leader.

We walked through a foyer and into a central patio that was open to the sky. Our intention was to visit Mother Teresa's tomb, which is located in the facility's dining room. But when we got there, we found out that the room was in use and we would not be allowed to go in until the ceremony was over.

We could see a group of about forty to fifty nuns seated, all dressed in the familiar habit that Mother Teresa had worn.

"What's going on in there?" I asked a nun passing by.

She smiled. "Today we are taking forty-five new members into our order," she said and then hurried away into another part of the building.

Since we were already running late and soon had to catch a plane, we couldn't stay. We looked around briefly and then left. As I walked out of the compound, through an alley, and among the throngs of people, I thought, *Mother Teresa would have been proud.* She was gone, but her legacy was continuing. She had made an impact on the world, and she had developed leaders who were carrying on her vision. And all appearances indicate that they will continue influencing people for generations to come. Mother Teresa's life is a vivid example of the Law of Legacy.

OBSERVE

Our ability as leaders will not be measured by the buildings we built, the institutions we established, or what our team accomplished during our tenure. You and I will be judged by how well the people we invested in carried on after we are gone. As baseball great Jackie Robinson observed, "A life isn't significant except for its impact on other lives."

1. *What was Mother Teresa's legacy?*

   _____

   _____

   _____

2. *How does Mother Teresa's work continue to impact others?*

   _____

   _____

   _____

3. *Why did the work of Mother Teresa continue after her death?*

_____

_____

_____

4. *What organization similar to your own has had a significant leader leave? How did this affect the organization? Why?*

_____

_____

_____

LEARN

If you desire to make an impact as a leader on a future generation, then I suggest that you become highly intentional about your legacy. I believe that every person leaves some kind of legacy. For some it's positive. For others it's negative. But here's what I know: we have a choice about what legacy we will leave, and we must work and be intentional to leave the legacy we want. Here's how:

1. KNOW THE LEGACY YOU WANT TO LEAVE

Most people simply accept their lives—they don't lead them. I believe that people need to be proactive about how they live, and I believe that is especially true for leaders. Grenville Kleiser, in his classic personal development book, *Training for Power and Leadership*, wrote,

> Your life is like a book. The title page is your name, the preface your introduction to the world. The pages are a daily record of your efforts, trials, pleasures, discouragements, and achievements. Day by day your thoughts and acts are being inscribed in your book of life. Hour by hour, the record is being made that must stand for all time. Once the word "finis" must be written, let it then be said

of your book that it is a record of noble purpose, generous service, and work well-done.

Someday people will summarize your life in a single sentence. My advice: pick it now!

2. LIVE THE LEGACY YOU WANT TO LEAVE

I believe that to have any credibility as a leader, you must live what you say you believe. (I've touched on that in the Law of Solid Ground and the Law of the Picture.) Because my legacy involves adding value by influencing leaders, I have focused most of my attention on leaders, and I have become highly intentional in my efforts to lead them.

I believe there are seven major areas of influence in society: religion, economics, government, family, media, education, and sports. In the early years of my career, I had influence in just one of those seven areas. I am constantly striving to reach and gain credibility in more of the others. I try to do that by building bridges, relating to people on a heart-to-heart level, and seeking to give more than I receive.

If you want to create a legacy, you need to live it first. You must become what you desire to see in others.

3. CHOOSE WHO WILL CARRY ON YOUR LEGACY

I don't know what you want to accomplish in life, but I can tell you this: a legacy lives on in people, not things. Max Depree, author of *Leadership Is an Art,* declared, "Succession is one of the key responsibilities of leadership." Yet the Law of Legacy is something that few leaders seem to practice. Too often leaders put their energy into organizations, buildings, systems, or other lifeless objects. But only people live on after we are gone. Everything else is temporary.

There is often a natural progression to how leaders develop in the area of legacy, starting with the desire to achieve:

Achievement comes when they do big things by themselves.
Success comes when they empower followers to do big things for them.
Significance comes when they develop leaders to do great things with them.
Legacy comes when they put leaders in position to do great things without them.

It's like my friend Chris Musgrove says, "Success is not measured by what you're leaving to, but by what you are leaving behind."

Truett Cathy, the founder of the Chick-fil-A restaurant chain, says, "Somebody told me, 'Truett, the determination of how good a fellow you are is the conduct of your grandchildren.' I said, 'Oh, don't tell me that. I thought I did pretty good on my three children; now I've got to see how my twelve grandchildren turn out.'"[1] Why would someone say you need to look at a person's grandchildren? Because it's a good indication of how the people to whom you have chosen to invest your legacy will carry on without you. For that reason, you must choose wisely.

4. MAKE SURE YOU PASS THE BATON

Tom Mullins, an excellent leader and former coach who sits on EQUIP's board, tells me that the most important part of a relay race is the place that's called the exchange zone. That's where the runners must pass the baton to their teammates. You can have the fastest runners in the world—each one a record setter—but if they blow the exchange, they lose the race. The same is true when it comes to the Law of Legacy. No matter how well you lead or how good your successor is, if you don't make sure you pass the baton, you will not leave the legacy you desire.

Tom knows this so well that for the last several years, he has been working on his succession plan. He began grooming his son Todd, who is also an excellent leader, to take the baton and lead in his place. As time has gone by, Todd has taken on more and more responsibility. Tom tells me that his greatest joy now comes from seeing Todd and other leaders step up and do an even better job of leading than he did.

Just about anybody can make an organization look good for a moment—by launching a flashy new program or product, drawing crowds to a big event, or slashing the budget to boost the bottom line. But leaders who leave a legacy take a different approach. They take the long view. Author, educator, and theologian Elton Trueblood wrote, "We have made at least a start in discovering the meaning in human life when we plant shade trees under which we know full well we will never sit." The best leaders lead today with tomorrow in mind by making sure they invest in leaders who will carry their legacy forward. Why? Because a leader's lasting value is measured by succession. That is the Law of Legacy.

DISCUSS

Answer the following questions and discuss your answers when you meet with your team.

1. *Why are leaders who practice the Law of Legacy rare?*

   _____

   _____

   _____

2. *Why does an organization need a team of good leader to succeed?*

   _____

   _____

   _____

3. *What does your organization's potential legacy look like? Who is involved in building that legacy?*

   _____

   _____

   _____

4. *What priority have you placed on mentoring others? Explain.*

   _____

   _____

   _____

5. *How would you go about choosing someone to replace yourself?*

   _____

   _____

   _____

6. *If you suddenly left your organization, what would the impact be?*

_____

_____

_____

7. *What will you do to ensure the legacy and future success of your organization?*

_____

_____

_____

APPLY

1. What do you want your legacy to be? If you are early in your leadership journey, I wouldn't expect you to have the definitive answer to that question yet. However, I still think there is value in your considering what you want your life to stand for.

Take some time to consider the big picture concerning *why* you lead. This will not be a quick process. The idea of legacy is closely related to a person's sense of purpose in life. Why are you here? What gifts and skills do you possess that relate to your highest potential as a human being? What unique opportunities do you possess based on your personal circumstances and what's happening in the world around you? Who might you be able to impact and what might you be able to accomplish as a leader in your lifetime?

2. Based on the ideas you developed concerning the legacy you want to leave, what must you change in the way you conduct yourself so that you *live* that legacy? Write them out. Your list may include behavioral changes, character development, education, working methods, relationship building style, and so on. Only by changing the way you live will you be able to create the legacy you want to leave.

3. In whom will you invest to carry on your legacy? Ideally, you should pick people with greater potential than your own who will be able to "stand on your shoulders" and do more than you did. Begin investing in them today.

TAKE ACTION

People invest in what they believe in. And if you are just half-hearted about the organization you work for, it is unlikely that you will invest in that organization's future. Spend at least an hour today brainstorming and recording your thoughts about why you do what you do. At the end of this time you may realize that you need to move into something that will better suit your gifts, talents, and the organization that you are willing to invest in. You may realize that you are right where you need to be, and that you should be investing in the vision and future of this organization. Or you may see how your current position is just a stepping-stone on your journey, but you can still invest by improving yourself as you try to strengthen the organization.

Some questions to get you started:

What does my organization provide for the community?

_____

_____

_____

Why is my organization important?

_____

_____

_____

I believe in my organization's mission statement because:

_____

_____

_____

The job that I think I would most enjoy would be:

_____

_____

_____

I do what I do because:

_____

_____

_____

When all is said and done, I want my impact to be:

_____

_____

_____

CONCLUSION

Everything Rises and Falls on Leadership

WELL, THERE YOU HAVE THEM—THE 21 IRREFUTABLE LAWS OF LEADER-ship. Learn them, take them to heart, and apply them to your life. If you follow them, people will follow you. I've been teaching leadership for more than thirty years now, and during those years I've told the people I've trained something that I'm now going to say to you: everything rises and falls on leadership. Some people don't believe me when I say that, but it's true. The more you try to do in life, the more you will find that leadership makes the difference. Any endeavor you can undertake that involves other people will live or die depending on the leadership. As you work to build your organization, remember this:

- Personnel determine the potential of the organization.
- Relationships determine the morale of the organization.
- Structure determines the size of the organization.
- Vision determines the direction of the organization.
- Leadership determines the success of the organization.

Now that you know the laws and understand them, practice them with your team. And take time to evaluate yourself regarding each of the laws using the evaluation tool on the next few pages. As I mentioned at the beginning of this workbook, nobody does all the laws well. That's why you need to build a team.

I wish you great leadership success. Pursue your dreams. Strive for excellence.

Become the person you were created to be. And accomplish all that you were put on this earth to do. Leadership will help you to do that. Learn to lead—not just for yourself, but for the people who follow you. And as you reach the highest levels, don't forget to take others with you to be the leaders of tomorrow.

APPENDIX

SUGGESTIONS FOR LEADERSHIP GROWTH

For many years I have written books to add value to people. Now that you and your team have completed the leadership evaluation, I encourage you to use the following resources to enable you to lead yourself and others more efficiently.

1. THE LAW OF THE LID
Leadership Ability Determines a Person's Level of Effectiveness

> *The 21 Indispensable Qualities of a Leader*
> *The Right to Lead*
> *The 360-Degree Leader*—Value #2: "Leaders Are Needed at Every
>   Level of the Organization" and Value #4: "Good Leaders in the
>   Middle Make Better Leaders at the Top"

2. THE LAW OF INFLUENCE
The True Measure of Leadership Is Influence—Nothing More, Nothing Less

> *Developing the Leader Within You*—Chapter 1: "The Definition of
>   Leadership: Influence"
> *The 360-Degree Leader*—Section I: "The Myths of Leading from the
>   Middle of an Organization" and Section II: "The Challenges 360-
>   Degree Leaders Face"
> *Winning with People*

3. The Law of Process
Leadership Develops Daily, Not in a Day

Today Matters

Your Road Map for Success—Chapter 5: "What Should I Pack in My Suitcase?"

The 360-Degree Leader—Lead-Up Principle #9: "Be Better Tomorrow
   Than You Are Today"

Leadership Promises for Every Day

The 21 Most Powerful Minutes in a Leader's Day

4. The Law of Navigation
Anyone Can Steer the Ship, but It Takes a Leader to Chart the Course

Developing the Leader Within You—Chapter 5: "The Quickest Way to
   Gain Leadership: Problem-Solving"

Thinking for a Change—Skill 2: "Unleash the Potential of Focused
   Thinking"; Skill 4: "Recognize the Importance of Realistic
   Thinking"; Skill 5: "Release the Power of Strategic Thinking"

Becoming a Person of Influence—Chapter 7: "Navigates for Other People"

5. The Law of Addition
Leaders Add Value by Serving Others

Today Matters—Chapter 12: "Today's Generosity Gives Me Significance"

Thinking for a Change—Skill 10: "Experience the Satisfaction of
   Unselfish Thinking"

Becoming a Person of Influence—Chapter 2: "Nurtures Other People"

The 360-Degree Leader—Lead-Up Principle #2: "Lighten Your
   Leader's Load"; Lead-Up Principle #3: "Be Willing to Do What
   Others Won't"; Lead-Across Principle #3: "Be a Friend";
   Lead-Across Principle #3: "Let the Best Idea Win"

Your Road Map for Success—Chapter 8: "Is It a Family Trip?" and
   Chapter 9: "Who Else Should I Take with Me?"

6. THE LAW OF SOLID GROUND
Trust Is the Foundation of Leadership

Developing the Leader Within You—Chapter 3: "The Most Important
   Ingredient of Leadership: Integrity"
Becoming a Person of Influence—Chapter 1: "Integrity with People"
The 360-Degree Leader—Lead-Up Principle #1: "Lead Yourself Exceptionally Well"
Ethics 101

7. THE LAW OF RESPECT
People Naturally Follow Leaders Stronger Than Themselves

Thinking for a Change—Skill 6: "Feel the Energy of Possibility Thinking"
Your Road Map for Success—Chapter 4: "How Do I Get There from Here?"
Winning with People
The 360-Degree Leader

8. THE LAW OF INTUITION
Leaders Evaluate Everything with a Leadership Bias

Thinking for a Change—Skill 8: "Question the Acceptance of Popular
   Thinking"and Skill 11: "Enjoy the Return of Bottom-Line Thinking"
The 360-Degree Leader
Leadership Gold (coming March 2008)

9. THE LAW OF MAGNETISM
Who You Are Is Who You Attract

Today Matters—Chapter 13: "Today's Values Give Me Direction"
The 360-Degree Leader—Lead-Across Principle #4: "Avoid Office
   Politics"
Talent Is Never Enough
The Choice Is Yours

10. THE LAW OF CONNECTION

Leaders Touch a Heart Before They Ask for a Hand

> *25 Ways to Win with People*
>
> *The 360-Degree Leader*—Lead-Up Principle #5: "Invest in Relational Chemistry"; Lead-Across Principle #1: "Understand, Practice, and Complete the Leadership Loop"; Lead-Down Principle #1: "Walk Slowly Through the Halls"; Lead-Down Principle #2: "See Everyone As a '10'"
>
> *Becoming a Person of Influence*—Chapter 8: "Connects with People"
>
> *Winning with People*

11. THE LAW OF THE INNER CIRCLE

A Leader's Potential Is Determined by Those Closest to Him

> *The 17 Indisputable Laws of Teamwork*
>
> *The 17 Essential Qualities of a Team Player*
>
> *Teamwork Makes the Dream Work*
>
> *The 360-Degree Leader*—Lead-Down Principle #4: "Place People in Their Strength Zones" and Lead-Down Principle #7: "Reward for Results"

12. THE LAW OF EMPOWERMENT

Only Secure Leaders Give Power to Others

> *Failing Forward*
>
> *The 360-Degree Leader*—Lead-Across Principle #7: "Don't Pretend You're Perfect"
>
> *Winning with People*—Section 1: "Are We Prepared for Relationships?"
>
> *Becoming a Person of Influence*—Chapter 9: "Empowers People"
>
> *Thinking for a Change*—Skill 9: "Encourage the Participation of Shared Thinking"
>
> *Your Road Map for Success*—Chapter 6: "How Do I Handle the Detours?"
>
> *The Difference Maker*

13. THE LAW OF THE PICTURE
People Do What People See

> *The 360-Degree Leader*—Lead-Down Principle #5: "Model the
> Behavior You Desire"
> *Developing the Leader Within You*—Chapter 6: "The Extra Plus in Leadership:
> Attitude" and Chapter 9: "The Price Tag of Leadership: Self-Discipline"
> *Your Road Map for Success*—Chapter 1: "The Journey Is More Fun if
> You Know Where You're Going" and Chapter 2: "How Far Can I Go?"

14. THE LAW OF BUY-IN
People Buy into the Leader, Then the Vision

> *Developing the Leader Within You*—Chapter 8: "The Indispensable
> Quality of Leadership: Vision"
> *Your Road Map for Success*—Chapter 3: "How Do I Get There from Here?"
> *25 Ways to Win with People*
> *Winning with People*

15. THE LAW OF VICTORY
Leaders Find a Way for the Team to Win

> *The 360-Degree Leader*—Lead-Up Principle #8: "Become a Go-To Player"
> *Thinking for a Change*—Skill 1: "Acquire the Wisdom of Big-Picture
> Thinking" and Skill 3: "Discover the Joy of Creative Thinking"
> *The Difference Maker*

16. THE LAW OF THE BIG MO
Momentum Is a Leader's Best Friend

> *Developing the Leader Within You*—Chapter 4: "The Ultimate Test
> of Leadership: Creating Positive Change"
> *The 360-Degree Leader*—Lead-Up Principle #4: "Do More Than Manage—
> Lead!" and Lead-Up Principle #8: "Become a Go-To Player"

17. The Law of Priorities
Leaders Understand That Activity Is Not Necessarily Accomplishment

Developing the Leader Within You—Chapter 2: "The Key to
   Leadership: Priorities"
Today Matters—Chapter 4: "Today's Priorities Give Me Focus"
Thinking for a Change—Chapter 5: "Unleash the Potential of   Focused
Thinking"
The 360-Degree Leader—Lead-Up Principle #1: "Lead Yourself
   Exceptionally Well"

18. The Law of Sacrifice
A Leader Must Give Up to Go Up

Developing the Leader Within You—Chapter 3: "The Most Important
   Ingredient of Leadership: Integrity"
Your Road Map for Success—Chapter 7: "Are We There Yet?"
Today Matters—Chapter 8: "Today's Commitment Gives Me
   Tenacity"
Ethics 101—Chapter 5: "Five Factors That Can 'Tarnish' the Golden
   Rule"

19. The Law of Timing
When to Lead Is As Important As What to Do and Where to Go

The 360-Degree Leader—Lead-Up Principle #6: "Be Prepared Every
   Time You Take Your Leader's Time" and Lead-Up Principle #7:
   "Know When to Push and When to Back Off"
Thinking for a Change—Chapter 3: "Master the Process of
   Intentional Thinking" and Skill 10: "Embrace the Lessons of
   Reflective Thinking"

20. The Law of Explosive Growth
To Add Growth, Lead Followers—To Multiply, Lead Leaders

21. The Law of Legacy

A Leader's Lasting Value Is Measured by Succession

NOTES

1. THE LAW OF THE LID
   1. "FAQs," McDonald's Canada, http://www.mcdonalds.ca/en/aboutus/faq.aspx, accessed 8 August 2006.

2. THE LAW OF INFLUENCE
   1. Paul F. Boller Jr., *Presidential Anecdotes* (New York: Penguin Books, 1981), 129.
   2. Thomas A. Stewart, "Brain Power: Who Owns It . . . How They Profit from It," *Fortune,* 17 March 1997, 105–6.

3. THE LAW OF PROCESS
   1. "The Champ," *Reader's Digest,* January 1972, 109.
   2. Milton Meltzer, *Theodore Roosevelt and His America* (New York: Franklin Watts, 1994).

4. THE LAW OF NAVIGATION
   1. *Forbes.*
   2. John C. Maxwell, *Thinking for a Change: 11 Ways Highly Successful People Approach Life and Work* (New York: Warner Books, 2003), 177–80.
   3. Jim Collins, *Good to Great: Why Some Companies Make the Leap . . . and Others Don't* (New York: Harper Business, 2001), 86.

5. THE LAW OF ADDITION
   1. Julie Schmit, "Costo Wins Loyalty with Bulky Margins," *USA Today,* 24 September 2004, http://www.keepmedia.com/pubs/USATODAY/2004/09/24/586747?extID= 10032&oliID=213, accessed 24 August 2006.
   2. Alan B. Goldberg and Bill Ritter, "Costco CEO Finds Pro-Worker Means Profitability," ABC News, 2 August 2006, http://abcnews.go.com/2020/Business/story?id=1362779, accessed 16 August 2006.
   3. Barbara Mackoff and Gary Wenet, *The Inner Work of Leaders: Leadership as a Habit of Mind* (New York: AMACOM, 2001), 5.
   4. Steven Greenhouse, "How Costco Became the Anti-Wal-Mart," *New York Times,* 17 July 2005, http://select.nytimes.com/search/restricted/article, accessed 22 August 2006.
   5. Goldberg and Ritter, "Costco CEO Finds Pro-Worker Means Profitability."

The 21 Irrefutable Laws of Leadership workbook

6. Greenhouse, "How Costco Became the Anti-Wal-Mart."
7. Matthew 25:31–40 *The Message.*

6. The Law of Solid Ground
1. Robert S. McNamara with Brian VanDeMark, *In Retrospect: The Tragedy and Lessons of Vietnam* (New York: Times Books, 1995).
2. Robert Shaw, "Tough Trust," *Leader to Leader,* Winter 1997, 46–54.
3. Russell Duncan, *Blue-Eyed Child of Fortune* (Athens: University of Georgia Press, 1992), 52–54.

7. The Law of Respect
1. M. W. Taylor, *Harriet Tubman* (New York: Chelsea House Publishers, 1991).
2. Based on the Bureau of Labor statistics, quoted in "Principal," Careers By the People, http://www.careersbythepeople.com/index/do/bio/, accessed 31 August 2006.

8. The Law of Intuition
1. Cathy Booth, "Steve's Job: Restart Apple," *Time,* 18 August 1997, 28–34.
2. Leander Kahney, "Inside Look at Birth of the iPod," *Wired,* 21 July 2004, http://www.wired.com/news/culture/0,64286-1.htm, accessed 1 September 2006.
3. Ana Letícia Sigvartsen, "Apple Might Have to Share iPod Profits," InfoSatellite.com, 8 March 2005, http://www.infosatellite.com/news/2005/03/a080305ipod.html, accessed 6 April 2006.
4. "iPod Helps Apple Quadruple Profit," BBC News, 10 December 2005, http://newsvote.bbc.co.uk, accessed 1 September 2006.

10. The Law of Connection
1. H. Norman Schwarzkopf, "Lessons in Leadership," vol. 12, no. 5.
2. H. Norman Schwarzkopf and Peter Petre, *It Doesn't Take a Hero* (New York: Bantam Books, 1992).
3. Kevin and Jackie Freiberg, *Nuts! Southwest Airlines' Crazy Recipe for Business* (New York: Broadway Books, 1996), 224.

11. The Law of the Inner Circle
1. Michael Specter, "The Long Ride: How Did Lance Armstrong Manage the Greatest Comeback in Sports History?" *New Yorker,* 15 July 2002, http://www.newyorker.com/printables/fact/020715fa_fact1, accessed 15 September 2006.
2. Dan Osipow, "Armstrong: 'I'm More Motivated Than Ever,'" *Pro Cycling,* 23 June 2005, http://team.discovery.com/news/062205tourteam_print.html, accessed 15 September 2006.
3. "Cycling FAQ: Learn More About Team Discovery," Discovery Channel Pro Cycling Team, http://team.discovery.com/index.html?path=tabs3, accessed 15 September 2006.
4. Warren Bennis, *Scarce Organizing Genius: The Secrets of Creative Collaboration.*
5. Proverbs 27:17 CEV.
6. Judith M. Bardwick, *In Praise of Good Business* (New York: John Wiley and Sons, 1988).

12. THE LAW OF EMPOWERMENT
1. Peter Collier and David Horowitz, *The Fords: An American Epic* (New York: Summit Books, 1987).
2. Lee Iacocca and William Novak, *Iacocca: An Autobiography* (New York: Bantam Books, 1984).
3. Lynne Joy McFarland, Larry E. Senn, and John R. Childress, *21st Century Leadership: Dialogues with 100 Top Leaders* (Los Angeles: Leadership Press, 1993), 64.

13. THE LAW OF THE PICTURE
1. Stephen E. Ambrose, *Band of Brothers* (New York: Simon and Schuster, 2001), 36.
2. Dick Winters with Cole C. Kingseed, *Beyond Band of Brothers: The War Memoirs of Major Dick Winters* (New York: Penguin, 2006), front flap copy.
3. Ambrose, *Band of Brothers,* 38.
4. Ibid., 95–96.
5. Winters, *Beyond Band of Brothers,* 283.
6. "Historian Stephen E. Ambrose, Author of 'Band of Brothers': The Story of Easy Company," Your Guide to U.S. Military, http://usmilitary.about.com/library/milinfo/bandofbrothers/ blbbambrose.htm, accessed 26 September 2006.
7. Author unknown, quoted in John Wooden with Steve Johnson, *Wooden: A Lifetime of Observations and Reflections On and Off the Court* (Chicago: Contemporary Books, 1997).
8. "Trouble Finding the Perfect Gift for Your Boss—How About a Little Respect?" 14 October 2003, Ajilon Office, http://www.ajilonoffice.com/articles/af_bossday_101403.asp, accessed 25 September 2006.

15. THE LAW OF VICTORY
1. James C. Humes, *The Wit and Wisdom of Winston Churchill* (New York: Harper Perennial, 1994), 114.
2. Ibid., 117.
3. Arthur Schlesinger Jr., "Franklin Delano Roosevelt," *Time,* 13 April 1998.

16. THE LAW OF THE BIG MO
1. Jay Mathews, *Escalante: The Best Teacher in America* (New York: Henry Holt, 1988).

17. THE LAW OF PRIORITIES
1. John Wooden and Jack Tobin, *They Call Me Coach* (Chicago: Contemporary Books, 1988).

18. THE LAW OF SACRIFICE
1. "Montgomery Improvement Association," King Encyclopedia, http://www.stanford.edu/ group/King/about_king/encyclopedia/MIA.html, accessed 8 November 2006.
2. "Chronology of Dr. Martin Luther King, Jr.," The King Center, http://www.thekingcenter.org/mlk/chronology.html, accessed 8 November 2006.
3. David Wallechinsky, *The Twentieth Century* (Boston: Little, Brown, 1995), 155.
4. Hillary Margolis, "A Whole New Set of Glitches for Digital's Robert Palmer," *Fortune,* 19 August 1996, 193–94.

19. THE LAW OF TIMING

1. David Oshinsky, "Hell and High Water," *New York Times,* 9 July 2006, http://www.nytimes.com/2006/07/09/books/review/09oshi.html?ei=5088&en= 4676642ee3fc7078&ex=1310097600&adxnnl=1&partner=rssnyt&emc=rss&adxnnlx= 1162847220-jiFf9bMhfwwKfuiWDA/Nrg, accessed 6 November 2006.

2. "New Orleans Mayor, Louisiana Governor Hold Press Conference" (transcript), CNN, aired 28 August 2005, 10:00 a.m. ET, http://transcripts.cnn.com/TRANSCRIPTS/ 0508/28/bn.04.html, accessed 6 November 2006.

3. Jonathan S. Landay, Alison Young, and Shannon McCaffrey, "Chertoff Delayed Federal Response, Memo Shows," McClatchy Washington Bureau, 13 September 2005, http://www.realcities.com/mld/krwashington/12637172.htm, accessed 2 November 2006.

4. "Red Cross: State Rebuffed Relief Efforts: Aid Organization Never Got into New Orleans, Officials say," CNN, 9 September 2005, http://www.cnn.com/2005/US/09/08/ katrina.redcross/index.html, accessed 2 November 2006.

5. Madeline Vann, "Search and Rescue," *Tulanian,* Summer 2006, http://www2.tulane.edu/ article_news_details.cfm?ArticleID=6752, accessed 7 November 2006.

6. "Hurricane Katrina," http://www.answers.com/topic/hurricane-katrina, accessed 7 November 2006.

7. Coleman Warner and Robert Travis Scott, "Where They Died," *Times-Picayune,* 23 October 2005, http://pqasb.pqarchiver.com/timespicayune/access/915268571.html?dids =915268571:915268571&FMT=ABS&FMTS=ABS:FT&date=Oct+23%2C+2005& author=Coleman+Warner+and+Robert+Travis+Scott+Staff+writers&pub=Times+ -+Picayune&edition=&startpage=01&desc=WHERE+THEY+DIED+, accessed 7 November 2006.

21. THE LAW OF LEGACY

1. Question and Answer Session with Truett Cathy and Dan Cathy, Exchange [Conference], 2 November 2005.